Inca Fo

Walking Tours Of Cusco

And The Sacred Valley Of Peru

Copyright Brien Foerster

Dedication

Firstly, I wish to acknowledge the Inca, a race of people of profound advancement for their time, when many other parts of the world, including Europe, were in the darkest of ages. Descended from a mysterious heritage that baffles all even to this day, they built the largest civilization in all of the Americas, until Spanish greed and ignorance blew out the flame of their life force.

To all of those that influenced my life, and helped learn what it is to be a human; part of the family of all humanity. I also thank all of my Ancestors for standing with me, and guiding my every move in life.

And for Irene, the love of my life...always there for me, and with me.

Chapters:

1: City Of Cusco (Cuzco, Qosqo)

2: Plaza de Armas

3: Stone of the 12 Angles

4: Coricancha: Courtyard of Gold

5: Tambo Machay

6: Puca Pucarra

7: Temples With No Names

8: Amaru Machay: Temple of the Snakes

9: Qenqo (Qenko)

10: Sachsayhuaman (Sachsa Uma)

11: Chinkana

12: Pisaq (Pisac)

13: Moray (Merey)

14: Salinas (Salt Ponds)

15: Chinchero

16: Ollantaytambo

17: Machu Picchu

18: Those That Dwell in the Mist

1: The City Of Cusco:

Cusco was the center of Inca culture, plain and simply. What started out as a small encampment of refugees from the area around Tiwanaku and Lake Titicaca, about the year 1200 AD, grew to become the capital of the largest civilization of the Americas by 1532; the year the Spaniard Francisco Pizarro arrived, with his some 160 "Conquistadors."

The "conquest" by this relatively small group of European mercenaries of Cusco in 1533 caused the rapid and irreversible decline in the fortunes and indeed fame of this beautiful indigenous city. As well as it's strategic importance.

It's name, Cusco, or Cuzco, and more properly Qosqo, is from the Quechua or Runa simi language, and means, by most accounts, navel, as in the place of origin. However, others, who have studied Quechua in detail believe that the name actually comes from it's founders, Manqo qapaq and Mama ocllo, observing a great bird that, upon landing, turned into stone, and that Qosqo is a species of large bird, not a condor though.

The "navel" idea does make sense, if it was used to mean "navel of origin of a new civilization." The idea that it means "bird turned to stone" is most likely a reference, in the scant oral traditions, to a younger brother of Manqo capac, Ayar cuchi, who supposedly was turned to stone here after fulfilling a monumental task.

Cusco was populated by other people when Manqo capac and Mama occlo arrived. The Lares, Poques, Sahuasiras and Alcabisas are four tribal tribal groups who are said to have inhabited the area of Cusco and the Sacred Valley at this time. Most of the early Spanish chronicles, and writings by Inca descendants from this time (16th and 17th centuries) state these early people were much more primitive than the Inca, in terms of agriculture and other "civilized" skills, and thus it was relatively easy for the Inca to rapidly gain positions of power over these earlier inhabitants, not so much through warfare, but through education.

Manco capac, the founder of Cusco, guided by the sun, called Inti

The Inca are said, from the above accounts, and oral traditions that still survive, to have originated near Lake Titicaca, as has been said, and most likely came from the area, just 10 miles south of the present day lakeshore, where we find Tiwanaku and Puma punku. It is known that these two sites, which are right next to each other but of different ages (Puma punku clearly being older) were constructed by highly advanced people, with amazing stone masonry skills.

The archaeological data, based upon limited analysis of the area, speculates that Puma punku began at about 1500 BC, and that Tiwanaku dates from a later time, perhaps around 300 AD. The work of Arthur Posnansky, a Bolivian engineer and archaeologist, who lived and worked at Tiwanaku (also called Tiahunaco) for 50 years, dated the site at somewhere around 13,000 years, based on the celestial alignment of the principle stones at the site. His work and legacy has been scoffed at ever since by mainstream archaeology, but has been supported by independent researchers such as Graham Hancock.

What is most intriguing about these two adjacent sites is that the constructions at Puma punku are of a higher precision than that of the later Tiwanaku; a point we will come back to many times in this book. It is as if, instead of the later society being more technically advanced, the reverse is true.

Entrance to the Kalasasaya Temple at Tiwanaku

What is clearly known is that the area was abandoned at about 900 AD, initially as the result of natural forces, which brought on human strife and conflict. An El Nino event, of 40 years duration, caused crop failure over this period of time. Weakened, the last of the priest kings of Tiwanaku were attacked by the Wari tribal people, and were forced to flee.

Here archaeological data and oral traditions confirm one another; but the mystery is not why they moved from here to the much more fertile area of the Sacred Valley of Peru to the north, but how they knew of it's existence. According to the legends and myths, the creator God Viracocha, who was personified as the Sun, named Inti, either sent Manqo capac and his wife (who was also his blood relation, perhaps sister) Mama Occlo, and three other related pairs of "brothers and sisters" down to earth, or made them to rise from the waters of Lake Titicaca.

They were commanded to go forth and create a new society. With a golden staff in one hand and a magical bird, in a cage in the other, they set of to find the new "promised land."

In reality, again, the first Inca, who were the descendants of the priest kings of Tiwanaku, seemingly took between 200 and 300 years to make it from Tiwanaku to Cusco and the Scared Valley. In the legends it says that the Creator told them that wherever the golden staff entered the soil and disappeared fro view, then that was where they were to establish their new home.

The exact location of this site is disputed to this day; some say that it is the Coricancha in Cusco, present location of the Church of Santa Domingo, while others say one or more nearby hills in Cusco. Even other informants suggest places in the Sacred Valley, just outside of the city.

And yet there are even more who suggest that areas of the Sacred Valley, especially the town of Ollantaytambo, were inhabited by the Inca, perhaps for a long period of time, prior to their establishing Cusco as their center.

In this book, I wish to introduce you to the most special, and often famous, locations, historically as well as aesthetically, in Cusco and the Sacred Valley. Every place in the book should be able to be visited over the course of 4 to 5 days, and I have included itinerary ideas so that you can tailor make your own journeys, based on the amount of time you have, and the depth of your interest.

A book like this allows you to become educated about what you are looking at without the need for a paid local guide; not that I am being disrespectful of their local knowledge, but why hire someone, make an appointment with them, and hope that they show up if you don't need to?

One point I will stress, however. No matter what any local person in Cusco or Peru tells you, the majority of the people who live there are not descendants of the Inca. An explosive statement you say? Not really. One of the best marketing ploys someone could give you, as a perspective guide, would be that they want to show you the "city that their ancestors, the Inca built." But in the vast majority of cases, as in more than 90 percent, easily, this simply isn't true.

A quick history lesson on the Inca civil war will help to explain this to you. What was paramount in the line of succession, from the first Inca, Manqo capac, to the last true sapa (high) Inca, Huayna capac (ruled from 1493 to 1527) was that the first born son always became the next high ruler, without exception. The logic behind this was that the sapa Inca was not simply a figure head monarch. He was the son of the Son, and as such had a "divine right to rule."

However, unlike European kings and queens, for example, he was more of a caretaker of his civilization, and not a dictatorial all powerful tyrant. And please also not that I used the term civilization, and not empire; a major distinction that I will get into later.

The sapa Inca was the highest decision maker on all affairs of state, including the government, military, and religious systems. However, although his word was final on all important decisions, he depended on consultation with experts in every field to give him the most current and logical advice.

He was therefore the absolute pinnacle of Inca society; and so his education had to begin in early childhood. It was thus important that a coherent system of succession existed, and from the first sapa Inca, Manqo Qapaq, that meant that the first born son would become the next sapa Inca.

Here is a list of the sapa Inca, and their supposed periods of rule:

Manco Capac   1200-1230

Sinchi Roca   1230-1260

LloqueYupanqui 1260-1290

Mayta Capac	1290-1320
Capac Yupanqui	1320-1350
Inca Roca	1350-1380
Yahuar Huacac	1380-1410
Viracocha	1410-1438
Pachacutec	1438 – 1471
Tupac Inca Yupanqui	1471 – 1493
Huayna Capac	1493 – 1527
Ninan Cuyochi	1527
Huascar	1527 – 1532
Atahualpa	1532 – 1533

This system worked well through the entire line of Incas, from Manqo qapaq until Huayna qapaq; through 11 sapa Inca and stretching from about 1200 AD until 1532. And then the unthinkable happened. Foreign diseases began to work their way, through the native populations, starting, most likely, in Panama during Huayna qapac's rule, which began in 1493 (a year after Columbus began his "discoveries" of the "New World.") Panama was one of the early Spanish bases, and the sailors and other personnel, probably unwittingly carried with them diseases from the "Old World" for which the natives of the Americas had no immunity.

Once the diseases, the most common and probably devastating one being small pox, reached Ecuador, Huayna capac, and his first born son, Ninan Cuyochi, were struck hard and rapidly. Ninan died first, and this left his father in a quandary; with the next sapa Inca now dead, and he himself quickly weakening from the disease, what was to become of his lineage?

It is said that Huayna qapaq had had visions and his sooth sayers had predicted that an outside force would come, during his reign, bringing devastating results to both he and the entire Tahuantinsuyu (Inca world, more properly being the "four corners or quarters of the land of the sun.) He had been told that there would only be a total of 12 sapa Incas. Now that Ninan Cuyochi was dead, it seemed that the prophesy had been fulfilled.

He decided, upon his death bed, to divide the Tahuantinsuyu into two parts; Quito (where he had been living for several years) and the area of present day Ecuador, which constituted his latest area of territorial annexation, was given to his son Atahuallpa, whose mother was of the royal family of the area. And the rest of the Tahuantinsuyu, south to Santiago de Chile, west to the Pacific Ocean, and east to the fringes of the Amazon basin, were to be held in trust (a more proper term than "ruled" by his second born son, of full Inca blood, Huascar, who lived, as was the tradition, in Cusco.

After Huayna capac's death, the two brothers lived in relative peace until about 1532 (morbidly coinciding with the time of the arrival of the Spanish conquistadors) when Atahuallpa decided to expand his control into Huascar's domain; the full story of this so-called civil war is described in detail in my book: A Brief History Of The Incas: from Rise, Through Reign To Ruin.

The short version of the story is this; Atahuallpa's forces, who were the greatest of the Inca armies, stationed in Quito as a result of Huayna qapaq's last phase of territorial expansion, moved south and captured Huascar. The latter was paraded through the streets of Cusco, bound, to show the power that Atahuallpa now had, and Huascar was held prisoner. Atahuallpa then summoned all of the Inca of full blood to Cusco, to discuss how now to properly re-organize the Tahuantinsuyu's state of affairs.

Lost of the royal family did indeed show up, for this was a confusing situation. Huayna qapaq was dead, the heir apparent, Ninan cuyochi was also dead. Huascar, next in line, was in prison, and Atahuallpa, the half-blood, seemd to be in control.

Atahuallpa had instructed his armies, while he was safely in Cajamarca to the north, to then kill every member of the Inca family down to four levels of relationship, which they did. This would insure that no Inca could possibly try, on the base of bloodline, to attempt overthrowing him on the basis of having a higher royal blood quantum.

The Spanish, a short time later, met with Atahuallpa in Cajamarca; they imprisoned him, and held him for a ransom in gold and silver. Huascar soon heard about the arrival of the Spanish, and attempted to contact them. After all, as the new and presumed true sapa Inca, he had access to far more gold and silver than did Atahuallpa, and was prepared to offer an even higher amount of these precious metals in return for his release.

Atahuallpa, through his spy network heard of his brother's plans, and secretly had him murdered. The Spanish in turn executed Atahuallpa, because they had now learned that he was not the highest Inca authority, and since they had now sacked the city of Cajamarca and surrounding area of its gold and silver, they planned to move south to the capital, Cusco. Atahuallpa had simply become a burden to them.

THE EXECUTION OF THE INCA.

Atahuallpa is spared being burned at the stake after "accepting Christinity."

I hope that this bit of a historical side track hasn't confused you; I included it here to show that very few Inca descendants exist now, almost 500 years after the deaths of Huana capac, Ninan cuyochi, Huascar, and Atahuallpa. So if a guide or resident of Cusco tries to tell you that they are of Inca descent, take it with a grain of salt.

So let us begin your tour of this royal Inca city.

As this is probably your first day in Cusco, some words of caution and health advice are very appropriate. If you have just flown in from Lima, please be aware of this one very important fact. You have just flown from sea level to an elevation of 10,912 ft., or 3326 meters in approximately one hour. Not only is the air thinner at this altitude, but the air pressure is lower, and if it is sunny, the ozone level much lower as well.

The best advice that anyone can give you as to what to do on your first day is…nothing. Rest, drink plenty of water, and read this book! By plenty of water I am suggesting 4 liters a day, throughout your stay. The thin air and intense sun makes the sweat on your skin evaporate at such a fast rate that you may think you are not perspiring at all. Also, coca tea, and chewing coca leaves can be very beneficial. The native people of this area have been chewing coca and drinking tea from it for thousands of years, so how can they be wrong.

Wear a hat? Yes. Sunblock? Of course.

If you are in good or at least reasonable physical shape, an afternoon outing may be what you want to do. If this is the case, the best place to start is the Plaza de Armas, which is the main square in Cusco, and has been so since before the arrival of the Spanish in 1533. Most of the hotels that cater to tourists, especially the "better" ones, those that are of 3 to 5 stars and have comfortable beds, hot water on demand, clean rooms, and staff that actually may speak English, are within 2 or 3 blocks of the Plaza de Armas.

I am not making fun of the people of Cusco in the above paragraph, but for a city whose main financial life line is tourism, and has been for more than a decade, a surprisingly small percentage speak much English. Anyway, let's get back to the Plaza de Armas.

View of the Plaza de Armas as photographed from the south side.

2: Plaza de Armas (Huacaypata)

The original Inca name of this square is the Huacaypata, or "place of weeping or meeting." It was originally twice the size it is presently, and was paved with small stones. Soil was brought back from any newly acquired territory, and a sample was deposited in the Huacaypata, to symbolize the unity of the Tahuantinsuyu.

Cusco's overall shape was designed in the form of a puma; one of the 3 major animals of spiritual and symbolic importance to the Inca, and indeed to their ancestors and other ancient cultures of the area. The puma represents strength as well as the conscious level of humans; the snake or serpent, which one frequently can see on true Inca walls, is wisdom and the subconscious, and the condor is the messenger of spirit to and from the Creator forces, representing the super conscious.

Sachsayhuaman, the great megalithic structure on the hill closest to Cusco, to the north, is the head of the great puma. The Coricancha, on top of which was built the church of Santa Domingo, to the southwest, is the genitalia or some say the tail of the puma. Avenida del Sol, one of the main thoroughfares, just to the west of Huacapata, is the outline of the spine of the puma, and Tullumayo Street, to the east, is the outline of the belly.

Huacaypata is the heart of the puma, both literally and symbolically. The four great roads that left Cusco into the four sectors of the Tahuantinsusyu, began (and in return ended) here. They were as follows:

Chinsasuysu: Northwest

Antisusyu: Northeast

Contisuyu: Southwest

Collasuyu: Southeast

In the present day, some sections of these ancient principle roads still exist, now being paved and inhabited more by cars and buses than Inca and llama! The same is true of the two major Inca roads, which went north and south, through Cusco, from Ecuador to Santiago de Chile. The coastal route is now the Panamerican Highway, and the more inland, Andes route unites major cities in the Peruvian highlands.

But let us return back to the Huacacaypata. In the center is a fountain, which I personally abhor. It seems to be a sculptural depiction of swans and Neptune like characters spouting water. What is it doing here, and how does this relate to the Inca? Oh, it doesn't. It was actually commissioned by the city of Arequipa , a city to the south, for it's central square. And the fountain that is presently in Arequipa was commissioned for the Huacapayta.

If you look northwards from here, you will see a large hill, with a massive white cross on top of it. Moving your eyes slightly to the left, you will see the outline of part of Sachsayhuaman, which we will get back to later.

If you look at the northwest corner of the square, the building on the immediate right is Inca; this was the palace of Pachacutec, the ninth sapa Inca. His name, sometimes written and pronounced as Pachacuti, means " he who shakes the earth." This is derived from the quechua words Pacha, meaning earth (as in Pachamama means mother earth) and cuti; to shake or turn over.

His name is very apt. During his "reign," he greatly expanded the Tahuantinsusyu, and, in fact, the true Tahuantinsuyu under this name began at this time. His campaigns resulted, by the time of his death, in the Tahuantinsuyu stretching from southern Ecuador in the north, to central Chile and Argentina to the south. He also conquered the Chankas, a war like group from the Apurimac area south of Cusco that threatened to attack the city, as well as the Chimu to the north, whose adobe city of Chan chan, near Trujillo, is a popular tourist destination.

It is also believed that Machu Picchu was built during Pachacutec's time, but I, and others who have studied the site in depth, think that he completed the construction, but did not build all of it. Certain areas and features, such as the Intihuatana (Hitching Post Of The Sun), Temple Of The Sun, and Temple Of The Condor seem to very much predate any of the Incas; but we will get more deeply into that in the chapter on Machu Picchu itself.

On the eastern side of the square is the cathedral, built right on top of the Palace of Viracocha, the eighth sapa Inca, and Pachacutec's father. The written accounts differ on the legacy of Viracocha; some say that he fought hard against the Chankas, who were later vanquished by Pachacutec, his son, while others state that he fled from Cusco when the Chankas were about to attack the city, and it was Pachacutec who deserves all honours in regard to saving the city from the invaders.

Cusco Cathedral; planted on top of the Palace of Viracocha

His name, however, was one that he chose, after having dreams of the Creator God or Spirit of the same name.

As you turn clockwise, and facing south, and to the left, at the entrance to Loreto Street, the wall on the right hand side was the Acllahuasi, or "House of the Virgins of the Sun." This is what could be commonly regarded as a convent, of sorts, but the role of the Virgins, and who they are, was somewhat different than that of nuns.

They were the most beautiful, intelligent, and artistically gifted young women chosen from throughout the Tahuantinsusyu to service the sapa Inca, so to speak. They were chosen at the age of between 8 and 10, and were kept in the Acllahuasi for between 6 and 7 nears, not being allowed to leave during this period. They were called Acllacuna, and were instructed by, and looked over by matrons, the Mamacuna, who instructed them in the arts of cooking, and weaving fine clothing and tapestries of vicuna hair, solely for use by the Inca, and his family.

The Coya pasca was the highest of the female priests, who oversaw the teaching of the Aclla cuna, and she was regarded as the earthly consort of the sun itself.

At this point, it is important to distinguish the Inca, who were the "children of the sun" from the Aclla cuna. It is most probable that the Coya pasca was of Inca pure blood, as were all in the highest positions of power in the Tahuantinsuyu, including the high priest, military heads, etc.

The first and principle wife of the sapa Inca was called the Coya, and it was only from her that the next sapa Inca could come. The sapa Inca commonly had many wives and consorts, some of whom could have been Virgins of the Sun, but only once they had come of a mature and proper age.

Next to this palace, just to the right, is the palace of Huayna capac, whom we spoke of earlier. At present the Iglesia la Compania de Jesus sits on top of the footprint of Huayna capac's palace. I say at present because earthquakes over the centuries have damaged it. It has been written that Huayna capac's residence was the most beautiful of all of the palaces; sadly, there is nothing left of it.

View of Cusco Cathedral and a rather inappropriately placed fountain

The majority of the churches and other colonial buildings in Cusco were made by simply recycling the walls of the Inca palaces. Close examination of any of the outer walls of any of the churches in the area will show you this, because the colonial walls are far inferior to the Inca ones in regard to the quality of the masonry.

It would seem that the Spanish simply took the Inca walls apart, one block at a time, and then rebuilt the walls, using a lot of cement/mortar. It was the use of so much mortar that has made the Spanish constructions vulnerable to earthquakes, because the soft cement/mortar crumbles easily when agitated by seismic movements.

The Inca walls, on the other hand, being made without mortar and incredibly tight-fitting, in many cases, resist any movement no matter how strong an earthquake is. They were designed with that in mind!

Well, as this is your first day in Cusco, you may be starting to feel the effects of the altitude and sun; or rain, depending upon what season you are visiting. It may be best to retire to your hotel, and continue your journey through Cusco tomorrow.

Our next place to visit, if you are still in the Plaza de Armas, or have come back here after a good rest, is towards the famous "12 sided stone." This is a must do for any visitor to Cusco, however, there is more to our little trip than just looking at a fancy rock and having your picture taken next to it.

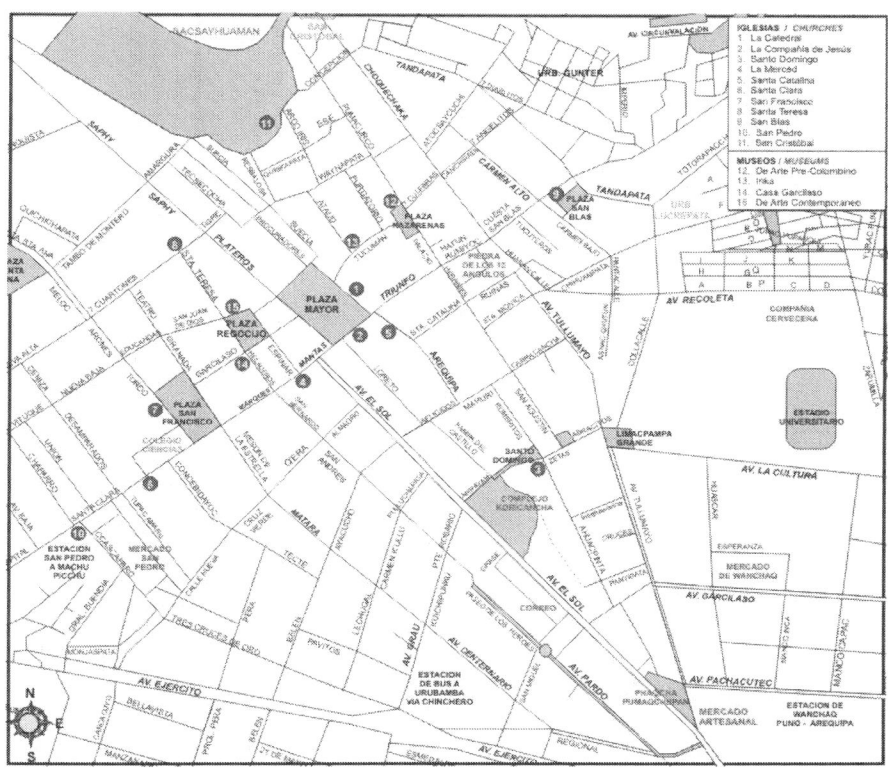

Modern tourist map of the city of Cusco

From the Plaza, go to the southeastern corner , and then walk straight, down Truinfo street, and walk a block; the Cathedral is on your left all the way down. Now, keep walking straight for another block (great shopping for antiques, clothes, and crafts on the right hand side of this block by the way.) And what remains of the Inca stone features of this side of the street are the remains of the palace of Capac yupanqui. He was the fifth sapa Inca, and ruled between 1320 and 1350. Little has been written about him, except that he was the first sapa Inca to take over and/or absorb territories outside of the Cusco/Sacred Valley area, and that he built many bridges and outposts in order to secure this expansion.

3: Stone of the 12 Angles

Now keep walking straight, cross the street, and you are now at the entrance of Hatun Rumiyoq street, a real Inca pathway! Notice the wall on your left, the way it is handsomely made from medium sized stones that fit very tightly together. I have honestly not been able to find out if this was a palace, and if so of whom, but it is clearly Inca in construction (no Spanish mortar or concrete to be found.)

The right hand side is the masterpiece; the wall of the Palace of Inca roca, the sixth sapa Inca. He was in power from 1350 to 1380, but, like Capac yupanqui, little is written of him. His greatest accomplishment was that he became the first Hanan sapa Inca, Hanan referring to the fact that he was in charge, for the first time, of all military, governmental, and religious aspects of life in the still wuite small Inca world. He is also said to have been responsible for creating major irrigation and perhaps water drainage systems in Cusco and the surrounding area, and "moved his palace" to where it now stands.

Hatun Rumiyoq Street: Down which you will find the "12 angled stone."

This may mean, that upon becoming the Hanan sapa Inca, he moved into the palace named after him, which could have existed prior to his rule. Indeed, as we delve more deeply into the subject, you will soon learn that many of the most spectacular and famous "Inca" stone structures may very well have not been made by the Inca.

The stone itself is green andesite, one of the hardest stones to be found in nature. It is harder than granite, and is a common stone in the area, though usually grey in colour.

About half way down the wall you will come to the famous "stone of 12 corners;" it is a remarkable engineering accomplishment, yet there is one at

Machu Picchu which has 32 corners! If you walk to the end of the block, you reach Choquechaka Street, which is the border of the Puma city, the belly street.

Directly across the street, on the left corner, is Jack's Café, a great hang out for expatriates from North America and Europe. And if you retrace your steps back and turn left (with the green Inca roca wall to your left hand side) there are other amazing features in the wall to explore.

About half way down this block, on your right hand side, is a pictograph in stone; the representation, in stone blocks of a puma, snake, and what is left of a condor. Any of the shop keepers will point them out to you, and you will undoubtedly find a local person or two there who can also show it to you. Please give them 1 or 2 Soles for their effort.

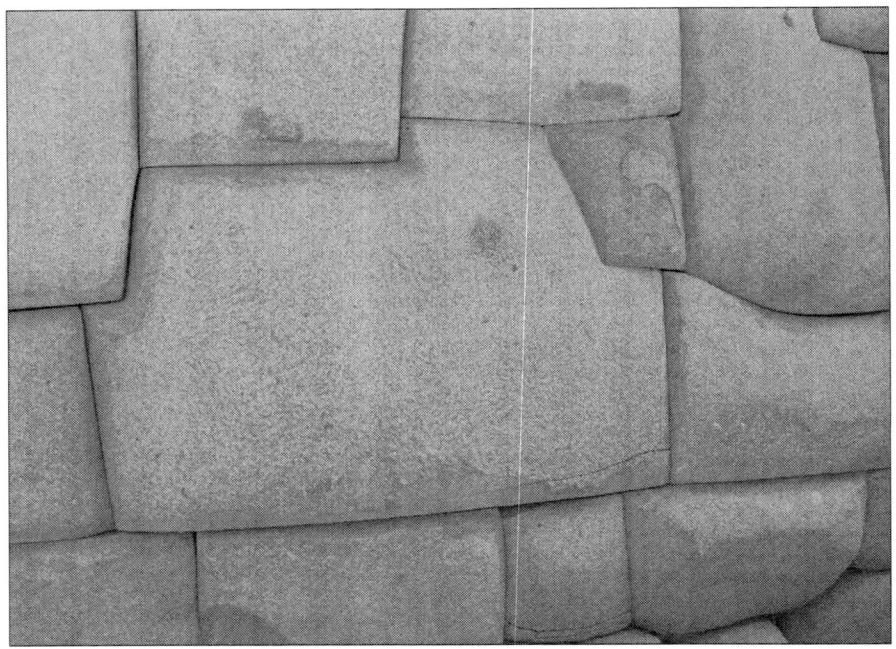

The face and eye of the Amaru (snake) on the east side of the Inca roca wall

What some may not know of, is that at the base of this wall, where it meets the pavement of cobble stones, you will see some small stones that tightly fit in between the larger ones. These are in fact "shims;" when an earthquake happens, these shims move out of the wall, allowing the edifice as a whole to move, as if it were one stone. Once the earthquake ended, the shims were shoved back into place.

You will also notice curious knob-like protrusions in many of the stones, starting about 4 feet up. Archaeologists say that these were sculpted on purpose to assist in the building of the wall; they allowed a rope to be wrapped around the block to be lifted, and the knob insured that the rope would not slip. The oral traditions, however, laugh at this idea. They say that the knobs are solar markers, used in ancient times to track the sun.

The original wall to the left, and the work of the "Incapables" to the right

As you walk around the next corner, another beautiful green andesite wall greets you. This one has been partially damaged by the Spanish, but what you can observe is how deep the beautiful joints between the stones extend into the wall.

When you reach the end of the block, have a look to your immediate right, and across the street. Here you will see Etnika's Shamanic Store, a good place to hire my native guide friend Jesus Merello.

Walking left, down Herrejas? St., go about 4 blocks until you reach the end, where Zetas intersects with it. Now, turn right. Walk one block (short and narrow) and stop; you are now at the epicentre of the Inca world; the Coricancha, or "Courtyard of Gold."

4: The Coricancha: Courtyard of Gold

The Coricancha was the spiritual heart of Cusco, and the entire Tahuantinsuyu. I am sure you are about to say "wait a second, you said that the Plaza de Armas was the center?" Well, think of the Plaza de Armas as the ceremonial and physical center, and the Coricancha as the spiritual/ethereal center.

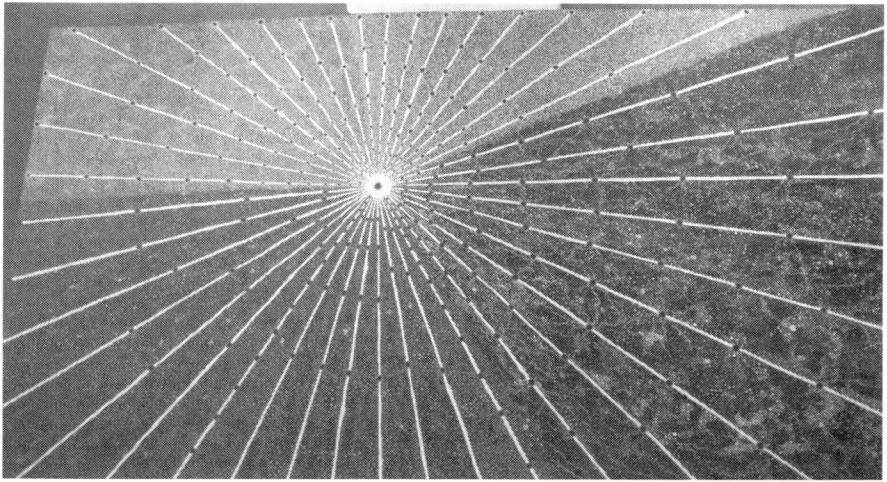

Map of the Ceque energy line system with the Coricancha as the center

This map, which you shall see inside, is made up of ceque lines. These are regarded as energy lines which radiate out from the Coricancha. The dots found along each ceque line represent Huaca, which are features in the landscape such as stone (natural or carved), springs, and mountain peaks. As the Inca believed, as many other cultures have, that all of creation is alive, a huaca could thus take many different forms.

Perhaps before entering the Coricancha, however, you may want to walk down Ahuacpinta St., to your left. On the left corner, stop a minute and have a look. Do you see the large green stone blocks like at the walls of Inca roca's palace? Next, look above them, and see that the stones are smaller and made of basalt, dark and grey. And around the corner you find even smaller and rougher stones. Do you think the same culture is responsible for three different styles of construction within this small area?

The difference in construction styles and time periods here is obvious

What you are looking at, researchers such as myself, Jan Peter de Jong, and Jesus Gamarra speculate is evidence of different cultures having lived in Cusco and the Sacred Valley. Those that shaped the green andesite stones, as well as the

Inca roca walls are known as the Uran Pacha period people, while the makers of the basalt sections and rougher stone walls made from smaller stones were the Ukan Pacha, now known as the Inca. We will get deeper into this as time, and your explorations continue.

Ahuacpinta Street is intriguing for many reasons. Again, conventional archaeology believes that all of the stone buildings in Cusco were constructed during the Inca period, from about 1200 AD to 1533. If this is the case, then why would such radically different building styles have been used?

The wall to your left, as you can see, is made up of very roughly shaped stones loosely fitted together, with clay mud as a mortar. On the right side, however, the wall, which is the original eastern side of the Coricancha, is made of andesite blocks that fit perfectly together. This is one of the finest examples of pre-industrial age stone wall building not only in Peru, but the world.

Western wall of the Coricancha

How can the archaeologists possibly think that these walls were made by the same people? And to add further to this, have a look at this set of three holes. The accuracy of the outer wall goes all the way to the inside, a distance of between 2 to three feet!

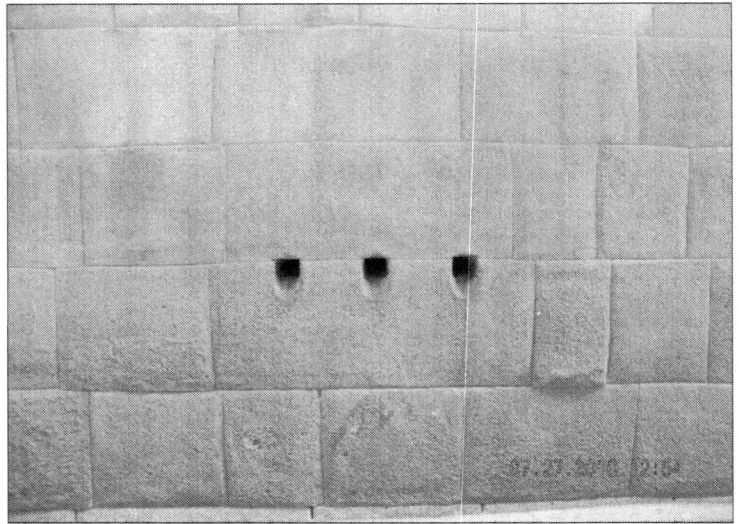

Water drainage holes? Or for acoustic purposes?

And now let us retrace our steps, and get ready to walk into the Coricancha. Once you are back at the corner, observe the large doors that are now a main entrance to the Church of Santa Domingo. This was once the site of the Temple of the Sun, the most sacred space in all of the Tahuantinsuyu.

What once was the Temple of the Sun, now a chapel

Such was the Spanish hatred of all things non-Christian, and the fact that by destroying the central place of veneration and worship to the sun god Inti, the residents of Cusco and the Tahuantinsuyu would become spiritually lost, they destroyed the Temple or House of the Sun to it's very foundation; nothing is left.

If you turn 180 degrees, and look down the narrow alley of Zetas, you are looking at an original Inca street. This one is important in terms of solar alignments, and was constructed for that purpose.

180 degree view from the last photo: sun rises here on the solstices.

At the solstices, the sun rises directly in alignment with this street, and in Inca times would strike a huge gold shield, on the western wall of the House of the Sun. The shine from the shield would be further enhanced by the fact that the southern and northern walls were completely sheeted in gold.

The ransom the last sapa Inca, Atahuallpa, was in part supplied by this gold; Pizarro's men, guided by Inca Chaski (runners) and carried aloft on royal litters, were carried from Cajamarca to Cusco. Once there, they tore, or more correctly had the sun priests tear, the gold sheets from the walls, and also removed the great shield and anything else made of silver and gold from the inner courtyard and other buildings.

The priests hands were broke and cut by the Spanish if the gold sheets were not removed quickly enough.

Inca sun shield symbol: notice the mouth has Puma teeth characteristics

Once you enter the Coricancha, and pay your ticket, observe the two magnificent rooms to your left. These are the Temples of Lightning, and Rainbow. Inside the first, aside from the magnificent stone work, you will see a real curiosity, in the center of the main wall. It is a tiny stone block, perhaps 1 cm by 1 cm in size. Was this a repair, or a humorous addition on the part of the makers?

These two magnificent inner buildings had been covered up and built upon by the Spanish when they built the Church of Santa Domingo on top of the Coricancha. An earthquake in 1950 brought this whole side of the church down, exposing the temples for the first time in many centuries. In their wisdom, and thankfully respect to the Inca, these two temples have been left exposed, for us to enjoy. As a Cusco joke says, "the great walls and foundations were built by the Inca, and the colonial buildings were constructed by the Inca-pables."

At the end of this long hall, you will find a scale model of what the Coricancha probably looked like prior to the "conquest." The entire top of the encircling wall was covered with a gold cap, perhaps 3 feet wide. This, of course, was stripped off and melted down by the Spanish.

What you will also find here are curious "orphaned" stone blocks, with interesting indents and shapes carved in and out of them. These were most likely found after the 1950? Earthquake, and have not been returned to where they originally resided. It is probable that they were parts of the constructions of the Coricancha which had been torn down by the Spanish as building material for either the Church of Santa Domingo, or other colonial buildings.

Joint systems such as this are also found at Tiwanaku and ancient Egypt.

What is most intriguing, to me at least, are the "T" shaped impressions on some of the stones. These, when two stones were aligned together, formed an "I" shaped depression, into which molten bronze was poured to help hold the stones, and thus the wall together during an earthquake. The only other examples of this technology in ancient times that I have heard of are at Tiwanku/Puma punku in Bolivia, Ollantaytambo in the Sacred Valley (which we will discuss in depth later) and in ancient Egypt.

If you look around this area, you will see a stone that has a perfectly round drill hole in it, about 1 inch in diameter. Anyway, please make your way into the central courtyard now.

The Coricancha, courtyard of gold was named after this central area. At the time of the arrival of the Spanish, it was a garden, but not one of plants and flowers that we normally think of, it was a garden of gold and silver. Life size human sculptures, animals, and plants, including full scale corn stalks adorned with gold and silvers ears of that vegetable, adorned the area. What became of all of this precious metal splendour and artisitic achievement? Yes, the Spanish took it all, and yes, melted most of it down into uniform ingots.

The reason why the gold and silver were so swiftly melted down, and by the Inca artisans who had made them, under duress, was that the Spanish were not an army sent by the Emperor Charles the Fifth as a specifically sanctioned and thought out enterprise, they were mercenaries; soldiers of fortune (and this is probably where the latter phrase comes from.)

The agreement that the Emperor had with Pizarro was that he would recognize their exploits in "New Castille" in exchange for 20? percent of the gold, silver, land, and people (yes people) that they found. The portion to go to the king was kept in its original form, to ensure that it had not been alloyed with cheaper metals, and this is thankful for us, because many of these masterworks still exist, albeit in Spain.

The rest was melted down to be immediately portioned out to the "conquistadors" who had "conquered" Cusco. Even the great gold plaque, in the symbolic center of the Inca world was not spared; it was gambled in a card game, and lost by the Spaniard who had been given it as his portion. That is where the Spanish phrase " He plays away the sun before sunrise" comes from.

You will notice a large stone, either basalt or andesite, in the center of the square, completely carved out; yes, this is one piece of stone. It has been supposedly brought here from another location, unknown to me, or others say that it has always been here. The function? Some say it is remarkably similar to the sarcophagus in the kings's chamber in the great pyramid at Giza, but, it is too small for a body to lay in, and only the most conventional of archaeologists and Egyptologists still think that the sarcophagus in Egypt is a burial place.

The solid andesite "box" that shows signs of real antiquity.

So this stone is a mystery, one of many you will see as you travel through the Inca world.

If you look across the courtyard, you will see what remains of the Temple Of The Moon, opposite the Lightning and Rainbow Temples. Like the House (or Temple) of the Sun, its walls were sheeted in metal, but silver, not gold. Gold symbolized the "tears of the sun" or "sweat of the sun" depending what stories you read, and silver was the "tears of the moon."

Where is the silver now? Yes, you guessed it. If you walk out of here and go to the left you will find a series of stairs, that lead to a "cat walk" which allows you to observe the Temple of the Moon from above. Look carefully at the top of the front wall. Going from right to left, you will see a series of bas relief rectangles. These then become circles, and then recessed lines. What were they for? The only reasonable argument I have heard is that they were used, in some way, as solar makers; when the sun tracked across the sky, they cast shadows which signified some relationship. Unfortunately we will never know, because there is now a roof over this whole structure; during Inca times it was open to the sky.

Curious circles in bas relief on the top of the Temple of the Moon.

Well, one more major feature to see. Once down the stairs and past the front of the Temple of the Moon, you will see a gold shield on the wall.

The "gold shield" in the Coricancha.

There is a description of what the symbols on this gold shield mean, but I for one takes them with a grain of salt. Another, possibly more plausible theory, and far more intriguing, is that of Wayne Herschel. Please check out www.thehiddenrecords.com for Wayne's analysis.

Our final stop in the Coricancha is outside, left of the shield. Walk down the hallway and through the large open door in front of you. You are now standing on the western side of the original Coricancha curved wall. Notice the strange protuberances, rectangular in nature. Again, these are believed by some, such as Jesus Gamarra, to be solar markers.

The curved wall of the west side of the Coricancha.

One final thing that is worth visiting is the tiny museum underneath the front lawn of the Coricancha, just to the right of where this photo was taken. It is included in the Boletico Touristico that will have purchased already, or will do in order to see Tambo machay, Puca pucarra, Qenqo, Sachsayhuaman, Pisaq and Ollantaytambo. This can also be bought at the museum.

The most interesting thing here are the elongated human skulls of the Inca, preserved behind glass. Conventional archaeologists will tell you that the elongation was the result of head binding, performed when the person was an infant, They do have drawings on the wall showing how this could have been performed, but I, for one, am not convinced.

Elongation is a world wide phenomenon, from Russia to pharaohnic Egypt, Africa, the Olmec culture of Mexico, North America, and elsewhere.

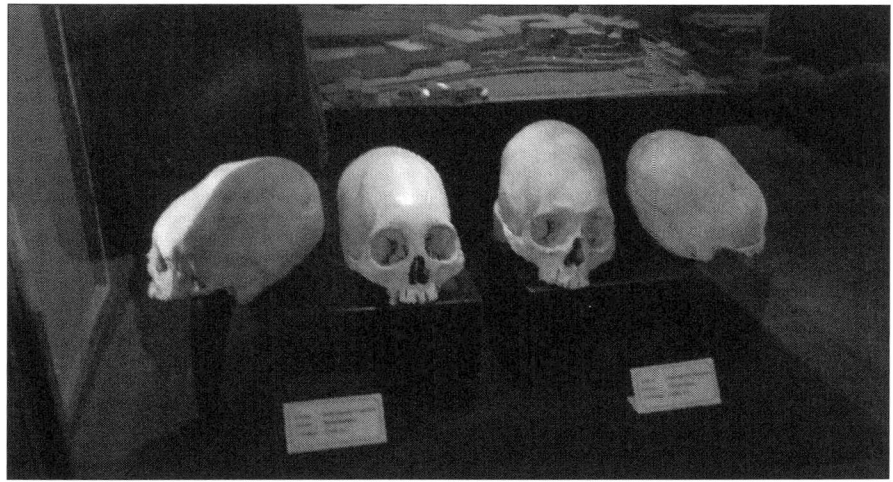

Elongated heads of the pure blood Inca.

Many old texts state that the Inca had heads of this shape; whether this was the result of binding, or that they naturally looked this way, is up to you to conclude. Since many skulls like this have been found at Tiwanaku, their homeland, it was a trait that dates back deep into history.

This ends our tour of the city of Cusco, and next will be go up the hill, to Sachsayhuaman and other great sites. Your Boleto Touristico does allow you access to various museums and some culture evening performances, please study it in order to make the most of this ticket.

5: Tambo Machay

The next tour is that of the area above the city of Cusco, to the north. We will begin at the farthest away site, within the area, and move back south, towards Cusco. If you are reasonably physically fit, this whole tour can be achieved within the space of one full day. If not, or simply don't want to see all of what is about to be presented, then simply scale back the number of sites.

Tambo machay is the first stop on this excursion. You can take a tour bus to it, or taxi, or even local bus (the one that goes to Pisaq.) The latter is clearly the cheapest way, and I am not going to quote prices here, because they of course tend to change, as do tour bus and taxi prices. The taxis are something that I will discuss here, at the beginning, because the prices tend to fluctuate dramatically, depending on where you are from, and how savy you are.

Everything in Peru, in general, is bartered, except restaurant food. And this especially applies to taxis, which are notorious for over-pricing tourists, especially Gringos and Gringas. There is a general assumption on the part of Peruvians that Gringos are all rich, and even have a bank machine inside their wallets that instantly produce money on demand.

For example, at the time of this writing, a tourist that shows up at the Cusco International Airport will be greeted by many taxi drivers, as soon as the tourist walks out of the main door. The average price that they want to charge you for the 10 minute ride to any hotel near the Plaza de Armas is between 12 and 15 Soles, whereas a local Peruvian will pay 4 or 5!

So if you are going to take a taxi to Tambo machay; always refuse the first quote; expect to pay at least 30 percent less. It is located about 8 km north of the Plaza de Armas.

Ritual bathing area of Tambo machay

The name derives from the Quechua (Runa simi) words Tambo, meaning house, and machay meaning cave, or possibly mach'ay, which is "to rest." I personally find it not to be the most interesting or well known of places, but what is good about this tour is that you will move, during the day, from the least to most intriguing of ancient sites.

Some researchers believe that Tambo machay was built by Inca Yupanqui (does not specify which one) as a hunting retreat, while there is more evidence, due to the running water that can be observed to this day that it was a ceremonial bath, for the Virgins of the Sun. There is a grotto about 500 m above the main terraces, from which Tambo machay derives its name.

The water in this fountain has been running for at least 500 years

6: Puca Pucarra

Across the street and less than a kilometre away from Tambo machay is Puca pucarra, which means "red fort" in Quechua (Runa simi.) It has also been called a prison as well, but that, like many "facts" about Inca places, is speculation. What makes the most sense is that Puca Pucarra was a military post combined with being a toll station; any products that came in or out of Cusco via this road, which is the traditional Inca trail leading to Pisaq in the Sacred Valley, had to pay a percent to the Inca for the use of the road system. The wares were stored there until they could be taken to Cusco or other centers for tabulation and distribution.

Here, as at Tambo machay, we see fine Inca wall construction. But if you look carefully, you can see strong evidence that older cultures preceded the Inca; Uran Pacha and Hanan Pacha.

Puca pucarra as seen from Tambo machay

Human face, from Hanan pacha period, in the center of the picture.

The entire backside of Puca Pucarra drops off into a small valley, as you can see, giving it a fort like appearance.

7: Temples With No Names

The next interesting feature is about 2 km away, which is downhill, so not too much effort is required. It is a house sized monument, of solid andesite stone, on the right hand side of the highway. Here you see many good examples of how large cubes of stone were extracted from the bedrock, as well as what appear to be steps and seats. The name of this structure is lost in the mist of history. Some archaeologists speculate that the Inca used these as small quarries, and yet, have no logical explanation of how the stone was removed.

The archaeological record, as scantily as it has been studied outside of the major Inca centers, shows that the only tolls in the Inca "tool kit" were round or oval stone hammers, wooden wedges, copper and bronze chisels, as well as sand and water used as polishing compounds.

The structure you are looking at, a huaca in Quechua (Runa simi) has many polished cut out areas, and no tool marks present, so how could the above tools have been used to extract the stone? A huaca is a place of veneration and worship; since the Inca believed that all things, including rocks, were alive, many may have been sculpted by them, or more probably ancestral cultures, to form small (and sometimes large, as we shall see) temples.

The temple like structure is right beside the highway; few ever look at it.

Jesus Gamarra has suggested that there are 5000 of these huaca in the Cusco/Sacred Valley area, and our next stop is to look at more of them!

Walk right across the highway from here, insuring that you don't get knocked over by a mad mini-bus (combi) driver, and go a few hundred yards toward Cusco until you see the obvious and easy entrance into a large cleared field. There is a well trod path on the right side of this field, which is what you want to be on. About 500 yards along, look to your left and you will see a bedrock clump in the field; this is another huaca, again un-named, but sculpted none the less.

Just a rock outcropping in the middle of a field?

No, it shows clear signs of having been shaped, a long time ago.

Flat surfaces that have clearly been sculpted.

Three photos of this may seem excessive, but it goes to show how much work has been done in the ancient past on one small stone outcrop of andesite. And if this seems to be in the middle of no where, then how many more are there?

8: Amaru Machay: The Snake Temple

As you keep walking along the trail, about now you will see a huge andesite boulder in the distance; this is the Amaru machay; the "Cave of the Serpents." Amaru is the Runa simi (dropping the term quechua from now on) word for serpent or snake, and the snake symbol is prevalent in Inca and older cultures. It is symbolic of the subconscious, and wisdom, whereas the puma is the conscious mind and the condor the super-conscious.

These three symbols and levels of conscious will come more into play the farther we travel on this journey of ours.

South side of Amaru machay (snake cave)

Entrance to the Inti (sun) cave on the left.

The Amaru machay, though called the "Cave of the Serpents" is far more interesting and complicated than that. In the above photo, on the left, is the Inti machay, or "Cave of the Sun", while to the right is the Quilla machay or the "Cave of the Moon" also called the Amaru machay.

Entrance to the Quilla (moon) cave guarded by stone snakes.

The "altar" directly below a hole in the ceiling.

View back at the entrance of the cave.

There are presently excavations happening on the south side of the structure, where the entrances to the two caves are, and sometimes this restricts or prohibits entrance. Do not be dissuaded however, security often becomes lax around 4 pm, and a kind word to the guardian (and a 10 Soles tip) can often bring good results (but I never said this!)

Of the two caves, the Amaru machay is the one most likely to be open for viewing. As you enter, notice the two snakes, bas reliefs, on the right wall as you enter. Also, by looking immediately to your left, where the wall meets the entrance, you will see the outline of a puma, and behind his tail, by a few feet, is an condor; the three most sacred of Inca and pre-Inca animal motifs.

Inside the cave, which is quite spacious, your eyes will be drawn to a hole in the ceiling, where light, whether from the sun or moon, can enter this dark space. The light dimly shines down on a smooth flat surface that could easily hold three or four prone people.

Hole in the ceiling, letting in sunlight and moonlight.

The cave, which most likely was a natural formation, has been shaped by humans; whether or not this was done by the Inca, or the Uran Pacha or Hanan Pacha is not known, but the latter two are most probable, taking into account all of the carved features on the top of and all sides of this immense stone outcrop which bear their mysterious "step" and "bench" hallmarks.

Were the caves places of meditation and/or worship? Clearly, but that is of course the easiest answer someone can give. The Amaru machay, also being called the Quilla machay, with reference to the moon, would clearly make it feminine, while the Inti machay would be sun oriented, or masculine. But why you would have a "sun cave" at all is odd; sun worship and reverence tend to be activities performed in the presence of that deity.

The probability that the first use of these structures pre-dates the existence of the Inca in Cusco and the Sacred Valley, later use by the Inca probably would have paralleled the most commonly held belief of the original use, that of meditation for pregnancy, or perhaps even birthing, taking into account the size of the slab inside.

However, we shall perhaps never know for sure, as the original builders, and their intentions and practices, disappeared millennia ago.

There are many other, somewhat smaller in the immediate vicinity of the Amaru machay "complex", especially near the eastern and north-eastern areas, and seem to be of the same age as most of the work done on and to Amaru machay.

A path going off to the west will take you, after about half a Km to the main road, and just before that you will see a series of "seats" in a stone just prior to reaching the road; this is Hanan Pacha again. It's name or function? Unknown. But once you read the road, and walk for a short while, you will see the outline of out next stop, Qenqo, also spelt Qenko or even Kenqo!

9: Qenqo

Qenqo seems to mean "labyrinth or zigzag" in Runa simi. It, like Amaru machay, is mainly composed of a very large sculpted stone, with natural tunnels and passageways that were later shaped; perhaps widened for ease of walking through. There are many large stone outcrops, which have been shaped, and a 4 m tall stone that greats you as you arrive.

The puma or frog edifice, lovingly surrounded by a stone wall.

It has been called by some a puma, and by others a frog. To me, it is a natural formation, and thus could be described as being either of the two. We have already discussed the symbolism of the puma, which we shall get deeper into as we progress, but the frog we have not discussed. Frogs, in the Inca culture have to do with water, since they are amphibians. It was believed that worship of the frog spirit would ensure that the rains would come in abundance from November through February, when they are still needed by Andean farmers to ensure the well being of their crops. Also, it would be thought of as a symbol of fertility.

This "sculpture" is surrounded by an intricate short wall, which could be of Inca, or possibly Uran Pacha construction. It is an example of a huaca, in this case natural, that was revered by the Inca and perhaps earlier people, to the extent that a seeming protective wall was built around it.

The main "body of the structure has many wonderful sculpted exterior surfaces, and passages.

Curious flat walls at Qenqo, which can not be natural.

Entrance to the Qenqo labyrinth on the left.

Inside the Qenqo labyrinth.

On a ritual level, Qenqo displays all three planes of human consciousness in material form. The upper surfaces are heavily sculpted, and represent the Hanan (super-conscious) level, the large passage way above is the Uran (conscious) level, and the deeper tunnel is the Ukan (subconscious.) Please don't get confused with the preceding terms, and the fact that the same words are used for the ages of the civilizations. Jesus Gamarra, who taught me how to identify the three ages uses these names, and I simply use them to honour Jesus, and I can't find better names to use!

The author inside the cave underneath Qenqo.

The large flat area where my head is resting is called a "sacrificial table" by most of the tour guides, a place where llama blood was collected for ritual use, or as a place to mummify bodies...even a place to store grain or make chichi corn beer. Wow, busy place. In truth, no one can give a truly well-fined answer, and the over use of the terms "ritual" or "meditative" space is enough to make you fall asleep. If the Inca spent so much time meditating and performing rituals, when did they have time to do anything else?

Zig zag channel used for predicting the future.

This, on the other hand, which is on the top surface of Qenqo, is clearly ritual in use. Some say that llama blood was used, while others say chicha, and the odd guide will foolishly say human blood; the Inca did not perform human sacrifice in this way. The theory is that the liquid was put into the circular area, and travelled through the zigzag channel. Depending whether it went left or right at the bottom would determine future events.

View of the sculpted surface of Qenqo as viewed from the south.

Imagine...all of this has been shaped? The reasons why are not known by anyone as far as I know. Conventional archaeology says that it is a rock quarry? Do you believe that? Not me. Aliens?

Anyway, there is no clear evidence that all of this work was done by the Inca, and so, perhaps it is too easy to say "earlier people did it with superior technology that has been lost to us." However, I have no other ideas to offer at this point, and no one else does, as far as I know.

10: Sachsayhuaman (Sachsa Uma)

We leave mystical and down right weird Qenqo behind and keep walking along the road to the last of our great sites in the immediate Cusco area; Sachsayhuaman. There are many other places that I know of, but some are off limits, either due to the fact that they are presently being excavated, or are so special to local spiritual Inca practitioners, that their space should not be invaded at this time; sorry.

Sachsayhuaman is a much larger and more interesting complex of areas than most tourist guides show, or even know about. To spend two hours here is frankly nothing, but that is how most guided tours are conducted, and I hate that. You will see the huge megalithic wall, probably be given mis-information about it, and then be shuttled off somewhere else.

This walking tour has no time limit; and the more time you spend, especially at Sachsayhuaman, the more you will know, and the more bizarre and complicated the place becomes.

View of the famous zig zag wall of Sachsa uma.

The name itself should be corrected at the beginning. Sachsayhuaman is a Spanish corruption of the original Runa simi name, which is closer to being Sachsa uma, meaning "furrowed puma." This refers to the fact that the zigzag wall represents the top of the head of the puma city of Cusco, while other drawings suggest that it represents the jaw of the puma.

Cusco: The city shaped like a puma, with Sachsa uma being the head.

You are entering the area coming from the northeast, whereas the more common approach for visitors is from the southwest; no big deal, both approaches lead directly to the large zigzag wall, for which Sachsa uma is most famous. Because this wall is so immense, and is made up of three levels or tiers, the description of it as being a fortress seems obvious, but is it correct?

The only clear reference that I have found stating that Sachsa uma had a military function was in 1536 when Manco inca, the younger brother of the last full blood Inca, Huascar, laid siege to Cusco by fire bombing the city from Sachsa uma. Manco had been installed by Pizarro as a puppet Inca, which he had rebelled against. So, much of the destruction of Cusco was as a result of Manco inca nad his followers trying to "burnt out" the Spanish occupation of the city. It didn't work, and Manco inca fled into the jungle area near Machu picchu, to a place called Vilcabamba, where he led guerrilla warfare against the Spanish until his capture and murder in 1545.

Prior to that, the age of Sachsa uma and its main purpose are hotly debated. Then concept of a fortress makes sense in that it is strategically positioned above the city, and so attack from the east, south and west could be observed from here. Also, one of the main road arteries, coming up from the Sacred Valley via Pisaq does pass right by the site.

The main problem is that so much of the original Sachas uma no longer exists, that a detailed study of it is now impossible; even the expert archaeologists have to do guess work here. From their perspective, in general, the Killka culture are believed to have first inhabited the area about 900 AD, 300 years before the proposed arrival of the Inca about 1200 AD. The Killka's presence is based on pottery fragments found in the general vicinity.

Notice how the size of the stones decrease with each level.

What is clear from the above photo is that the zigzag wall is composed of three levels, with the stones decreasing in size on each successive level. The only reason why any of it is still intact is that the stones that still exist there tended to be too large for the Spanish to move.

Following the siege of Cuzco, the Spaniards began to use Sachsa uma as a source of stones for building Spanish Cuzco and within a few years much of the complex was demolished. The site was destroyed block-by-block to build the new governmental and religious buildings of the city, as well as the houses of the wealthiest Spaniards. In the words of Garcilaso de la Vega, who was an author and descendant of the Inca in the 16th century: "to save themselves the expense, effort and delay with which the Indians worked the stone, they pulled down all the smooth masonry in the walls. There is indeed not a house in the city that has not been made of this stone, or at least the houses built by the Spaniards."

The lowest level of the wall is where we find many of the largest sculpted stones in Cusco and the Sacred Valley. Estimates of their weight vary wildly, but some are in the area of 100 tons; and indeed, as you can see, not a piece of paper nor human hair can fit in between many of the joints.

The author dwarfed by one of the larger limestone rocks.

Theories as to how these walls were put together vary from the building of wooden tripods to lower the upper stones down to fit into the lower ones, to the making of full size plaster models; both of which I find silly. Why not simply say that we don't know? And listen to the early Inca informants who state that Sachsa uma was there when the Inca arrived, built by an earlier people, the Uran Pacha and/or Hanan Pacha?

There were stone towers that once sat proudly on the upper level of the top tier of the zigzag wall. Sadly, just the outline of the foundation of one still exists. It is said to have been up to forty feet high, and was sheeted in pure gold. From this area you have great views of the entire city of Cusco below.

Panorama of Cusco from atop Sahsa uma.

Base of the greatest of towers at Sachsa uma; the tower and gold covering are now gone.

The expansive open court to the north side of the zigzag wall is now where the festival of Inti raymi is held, on the 24th of June. This was originally conducted in the Plaza de Armas, as we have read at the beginning of the book, and is a huge tourist draw. Traditionally, Inti raymi celebrates the winter solstice, and the time of the rebirth of the sun Inti, the source of all life. In turn, the Inca, being the "Children of the Sun" were and are also celebrated at this time, and the events lasted nine days, including plays and songs recounting the arrival of the first Inca to Cusco.

Inti raymi celebration with the Sapa Inca being carried aloft.

The Inti raymi was banished by the Spanish authorities in 1535 (for obvious reasons) and was not performed again until 1944! Now let us move northwards, to more intriguing mysteries, many of whom are not shown by most tour guides.

The "Inca Thrones" north of the zig zag wall.

You will find this amazing feature on the northeast side of the large stone outcrop on the north side of the open space you are now standing on. The conventional description is that these are "Inca Thrones" where the royal family would sit to watch over events occurring on the parade grounds below. What? Then why do these "thrones" face east, and not south, which they would do if the grounds below were to be looked at with any degree of comfort.

Sitting here (which you could do if it wasn't roped off) your gaze would naturally focus on the great mountain of Ausengate, one of the great Apu, or spirit mountains. Ausengate is where the last of the great spiritual keepers of Inca traditions live in any number. It is believed that they escaped during the Spanish invasion and went to live high up Ausengate, where they have been ever since. However, to say that they are genetic Inca descendants is doubtful.

Anyway, back to the stone "steps." What are they, and who made them? The lack of tool marks, and the exacting polished surfaces again lead me to believe that they pre-date the Inca, and were made by the Uran or Hanan Pacha cultures.

"Inca Slides" are ancient folds of andesite stone.

Further along (not far) you will see this feature, called the "Inca Slide." It is a natural andesite outcrop which through geologic time twisted and turned so that the stratified layers are now 90 degrees from when they would have been originally made by the earth. The grooves are the result of weathering over millions of years, and the steps that we just looked at are part of the same stone edifice.

Some guides say that the "slides" were a place of young Inca warrior or prince initiation, but I for one doubt that.

And now we enter the area which is perhaps the most intriguing part of the Sachsa uma area, and the least explained, and the most "covered up" (excuse the pun.) This first area is called the Inca graveyard, because skeletons were found here, and it has only been recently excavated. However, it is the abundance of clearly shaped andesite stone outcrops that is quite amazing to me, and others who are looking for evidence of the Uran Pacha and Hanan Pacha cultures' legacy.

Hanan pacha shaped stone at the entrance to the "cemetery."

This is just one one many carved surfaces that you will see here. This stone is at the entrance to the slightly sunken "graveyard."

One of hundreds of Huaca in the area.

Another example of a huaca in the area, which like I have said, there are hundreds. Beyond here you will find a large circular depression in the earth. Some say that was an Inca festival and or performance space. What is curious about it is that at the northeastern edge you will find the entrance to a tunnel, called a Chinkana in Runa simi.

The round stadium like area north of the zig zag wall.

You can walk through this Chinkana relatively easily, and quite upright most of the way; it takes about a minute or two. But beware, it is pitch black, and so it is easy to hit your head against the walls, or heads of other people coming the other way. It's function has been lost, but some suggest that it served as an entrance by performers into the great circle, or as a drain for when the circle was filled with water for esoteric purposes!

11: The Chinkana

A reasonably short walk farther to the north (northeastish) brings you one of my favourite places, called the Chinkana. Now I know that I just used the word chinkana to refer to a tunnel, and this appears to be a huge rock, but both are accurate uses of the term; let me explain. On the northeastern area of this massive sculpted outcrop you will find a large stone slab, containing a stairway, which has fallen off of the main mass. When this occurred is debated, but most likely after the arrival of the Spanish.

Western side of the Chinkana; solid andesite.

The three "Inca Thrones" on the north side of the Chinkana.

The fallen section has closed off what researchers, using ground penetrating have found to be a tunnel (chinkana) with stairs, about 100 of them, going down to a flat area. From there it id believed, from oral traditions, that the chinkana continues down, on a gradual slope, to Cusco itself, going under the Plaza de Armas and surfacing at the Coricancha. Due to government "red tape" and fears that researchers would either get lost or hurt exploring this chinkana from either end, entry is completely prohibited.

Eastern side of the Chinkana; the broken off section hides the tunnel entrance.

This more or less ends the tour of the Sachsa uma area; there are Inca baths and many other interesting small places of interest to be found here. If you wish to explore further, contact Hector Contraras Zuniga for a complete tour. He grew up right next to Sachsa uma, and knows it better than anyone that I have ever met. His contact information is at the back of the book.

12: Pisaq (or Pisac)

The market town of Pisaq (also spelled Pisac) is our next stop; but not on foot. It is located about an hour's drive from the Plaza de Armas in Cusco, and is in the Sacred Valley. The cheapest way to get there is by local bus, or you can take a combi or taxi if you want to get there faster.

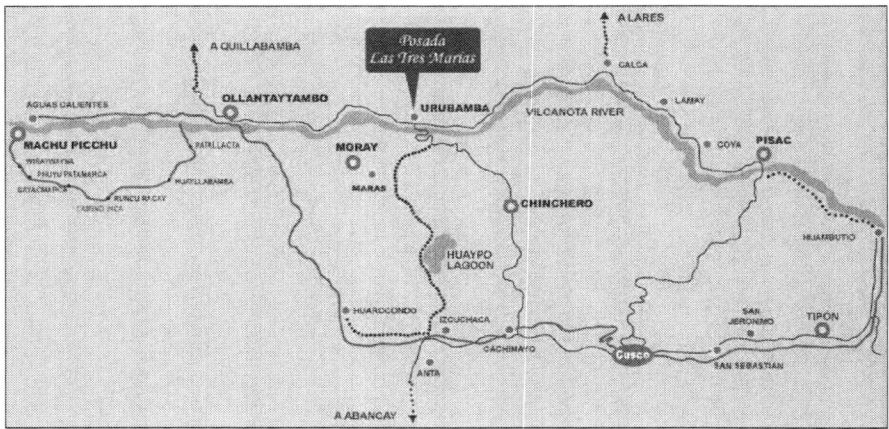

Map of the Sacred Valley.

Located directly above the market town are the remains of Inca Pisaq. The Spanish explorer Francisco Pizarro and the conquistadores destroyed Inca Písaq in the early 1530s. The modern town of Písaq was built in the valley by Viceroy Toledo during the 1570s. The market here is open 7 days a week, contrary to what other sources may tell you, and is one of the best, if not the best in the area.

Looking down into the Sacred Valley from the highway to Pisaq.

The terraces or Andene above Pisaq make the shape of a huge condor.

The agricultural terracing system that rises up above the town, and ends where the ruins of Inca Pisaq begin, forms the shape of a huge condor. It is probable that the Inca constructed most if not all of this andena (Runa simi for terraces) system, as are the vast majority of the andena in the Sacred Valley area, to feed a large and growing population. And yes, the name Andes (as in the mountains) comes from this term.

Inca Pisaq (I hate the term "ruins") with military, religious, and agricultural structures, served at least a triple purpose. Researchers believe that it defended the southern entrance to the Sacred Valley, while Choquequirqo defended the western entrance, and the fortress at Ollantaytambo the northern. Inca Pisaq controlled a route which connected the Inca Empire with the border of the rain forest. You need to either take a taxi or tour bus up to the site; walking would take more than an hour of steep hiking.

Your first view will be of magnificent andene that will be right in front of you. To your right and up a little, are major building constructions, and the rest are beyond the andene, and off to the right and upwards.

View of the andene and Vilcamayu River at the entrance to Inca Pisaq.

The ruins are separated along the ridge into four groups: Pisaqa, Intihuatana, Q'allaqasa, and Kinchiracay. Intihuatana (the Temple of the Sun) includes a number of baths and temples. The Intihuatana, a volcanic outcrop carved into a "hitching post" for the Sun (or Inti), is the focus of the complex.

The first complex that you may wish to explore is a bit of a trek, but well worth it. On the right, on the side of the hill just before entering this area you will see quite a number of small caves; these are tombs, probably Inca, that have all been plundered.

The urban cluster of buildings at Pisaq.

After visiting this area, you can either back track down to where the andene are; or follow paths over the higher hills; most will back track, which may be a smart decision. On my first trip I took the other route with my guide friend Jesus Merello, and it was somewhat perilous.

Stone staircases leading up to the Intihuatana area.

The above photo looks more difficult than it is, but in order to reach the Intihuatana, climbing is required. Off to your left, you will get great views of the Vilcanota (Vilcamayu) River, the life blood of the Sacred Valley, and other wonders of the natural and man-made worlds, living in as much harmony as a Japanese garden.

Complex of farmer's buildings near the terraces.

The Intihuatana surrounded by an Uran pacha wall.

The Intihuatana is not as impressive perhaps as the one at Machu picchu, in terms of size and shape, but part of this is due to the Spanish having damaged it soon after their arrival. What may be most interesting about this area is that, like in the photo above, we see evidence that an earlier culture was at work. The wall in the foreground intricately wraps around and embraces the Intihuatana, which, like the one at Machu picchu was made from exposed bedrock. It seems from this an many other examples in the Sacred Valley that the Inca built such walls around constructions made by the Uran and Hanan Pacha cultures, out of reverence.

Behind you, as you look at this, is another exposed stone which seems to be an Intihuatana, but is blocked in by two later walls, so can no longer function as a solar calendar; further evidence of different periods on construction, across a time line of much more than 1200 AD to 1533.

You will also notice fountains and water channels that still function; these date back to at least the Inca period, if not earlier. If you wish to travel even higher up, there are more enticing constructions to amaze you.

View overlooking the Intihuatana area.

The walk back to the bus or taxi you got out of is fine, but if you have a little more energy in you, a path and stair system weave off to the right, back down where the Intihuatana is, and will take you back to Pisaq market; well worth the effort.

The pathway down from Inca Pisaq to the town of Pisaq.

The area from Pisaq to Ollantaytambo, along the floor of the Sacred Valley and winding along the side of the Vilcamayu River, has some Inca sites, but none of which I think are worth stopping to see. Instead, let us move along, whether by bus or taxi, back to Cusco. But not the way we came. Instead, travel to the town of Urubamba, and then catch another bus (or tell your taxi driver) that you want to go to Moray, which is on the way to Maras (a small town) above the Sacred Valley.

The Sacred Valley looking north towards Ollantaytambo.

One note about the Vicanota/Vilcamayu River. Traditionally, it is called the Vilcanota from it's source in the Andes until it reaches the town of Urubamba, where it's name changes to the Urubamba River. This is kind of important, because once you reach Machu picchu (not today!) any guide or other reference material that you read will probably name the river at the base of Machu picchu as the Urubamba or possibly the Vilcamayu.

In the most traditional sense, the entire length of this river, from its Andean source to where it joins the Ucayali, downstream from Machu picchu, is the Vilcamayu, meaning sacred river in Runa simi. The Ucayali then joins the Amazon at Iquitos, in the northern jungle of Peru, which eventually empties into the Atlantic Ocean.

13: Moray (Merey)

You ascend out of Urubamba as you head towards Moray, and notice how the ascent causes the environment to gradually become drier. Gone are the huge fields of traditional maize of the Sacred Valley, and hello to potato (papa) fields.

Moray is far larger and more spectacular than most photographs can capture, and it's original function mysterious.

The main sunken "amphitheatre" of Moray.

Moray (also spelled and pronounced Merey) is said to have been an Inca agricultural experimental station. Since crops, as you have seen the Sacred Valley were grown from the valley floor to the tops of the mountains in Andene, it is logical that the Inca wished to experiment on what crops, and crop varieties would be best suited for different altitudes, soil conditions, rainfall, etc.

More than 200 varieties of potatoes (some say 2000) were developed within the sphere of Inca influence (not necessarily by them alone, but also by the different groups that became absorbed into the Tahuantinsuyu) as well as numerous varieties of corn, beans, peppers, squash, etc.

Some of the over 200 varieties of potatoes still cultivated in Peru.

Seeds cultivated at this site were likely sent throughout the Incan empire to improve yield in the harsh conditions of the Andes and were probably one of the benefits offered by the Incas for peaceful incorporation of neighbouring tribes into the Incan empire. Today the site is a series of co-centric circles on plateau´s 400m above the valley floor (3,200-3,500m above sea level). The site was designed by the Incas to take advantage of natural depressions below the level plain and model andean, jungle and semi-tropical environments for the growth of different plant varieties. Pollen studies indicate that soils from each of these regions was imported by the incas to each of the large circular basins. In the largest of the depressions (150m) a serious of water channels can be seen finding their way to the bottom. Studies have found temperature variations up to 5 degrees Celsius; same research says more.

There are actually 3 large circular depressions that make up the Moray site, though most photos only show one.

The three amphitheatre/agricultural stations of Moray.

They appear to have been natural, perhaps volcanic depressions, which were later sculpted for their agricultural use.

But what about before the Inca? Is it possible that the Uran or Hanan Pacha cultures also used this site, as an agricultural station, or something else? Every August 1 (or so) a major Inca festival occurs here. It is the Festival de Pachamama, which is a celebration of Mother Earth (Pachamama) dating back to at least Inca times. An all day event, it features the presentation of officials and military from the four regions of the Tahuantinsuyu, ritual cleansing of the area and especially lowest circular "stage" by the Virgins of the Sun, and a grand speech by the sapa Inca, as well as the burning of a food offering to Pachamama herself by the high Priest.

Musicians at the August Celebration of Pachamama Festival.

Representatives of the different Suyus (districts) of the Tahuantinsuyu and the flag.

Virgins of the Sun in the central circle at the Festival Of Pachamama.

The Sapa Inca making a pronouncement to the crowd.

The high priest preparing the offering (Despacho) to Pachamama.

The acoustics in this, the largest of the three circular terrace systems, is amazing. It is highly likely that this Pachamama ritual was conducted during this fallow period of the Inca agricultural year, when the land was allowed to rest, out of gratitude for all of the food that Pachamama had provided that year. But whether or not this ceremony predates the Inca, and indeed the structures themselves, is unclear.

14: Salinas Salt Flats

Next, as we move back towards Cusco, we will stop at the Salinas salt flats, which is a surface salt mine, used by the Inca for centuries, and quite possibly by others earlier than that. I know that I keep seemingly always saying or suggesting that practically everything may have had a use before the time of the Inca. I mean in no way to diminish the amazing feats and accomplishments by them, but since it is clear that they were not the first occupants of Cusco or the Sacred Valley, it is probable that they inherited many things, such as the salt mine.

View from the entrance to Salinas.

View of the salt flats of Salinas from a nearby hill.

The salt emerges as hot salt water from the side of a hill, and follows a series of channels, gradually filling the 3000 plus pools that make up this site. Once a pool is full, the entry of further water is blocked by a stone. The heat of the sun then gradually evaporates the water out, which takes about a month, depending on the season.

Worker at Salinas in one of the thousands of drying ponds.

15: Chinchero

Our last stop for the day is Chinchero, located along the main road back towards Cusco. Do not be discouraged by the look of this place once you enter it; there does not seem to be anything special about Chinchero, and I have driven past many times. However, the Inca and older structures up near the main church are both substantial and mesmerizing.

Street with craft vendors on the way up to the Inca area of Chinchero.

Chinchero was where Inca Tupaq Yupanqui made his country residence. It was common for many if not all of the sapa Inca to have a residence outside of Cusco, perhaps to get away from the affairs of state and activity of the capital, which had a population of at least 250,000 at the time of the Spanish Conquest.

As you enter the main square, with the church in front of you, walk immediately to your left and look down. In the grass you should be able to make out the pattern that the images below show you.

Inca or pre-Inca oracle channel for predicting the future.

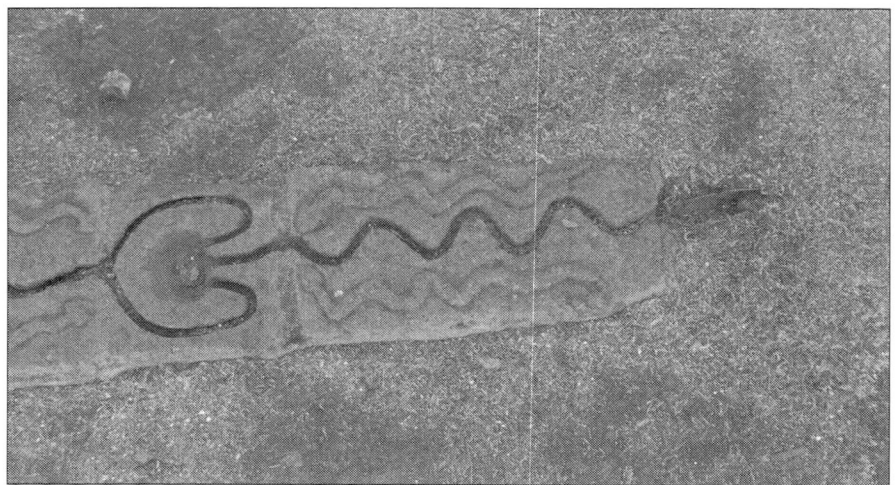

Notice the Amaru (snakes) and the channels that divide the flowing liquid.

Careful examination of this "trough" will show relief carved snakes, a frog, a puma, and a condor. As has been previously discussed, the snake is wisdom of the subconscious, the puma the conscious mind, the condor the super-conscious, and the frog a symbol of fertility and cycles of precipitation. This probably had the same function as the "trough" that we saw at Qenqo; in this case, chicha or llama blood was poured onto the large rock on the left hand side of the first of the two photos, and entered the little pool on the ground. From there it traveled to the right, and had to enter one of two branch channels. Predicting the future? That is what I propose.

Inca or possibly Uran pacha wall with Inca style trapezoidal niches.

These large niches are of the classic Inca style, called trapezoidal by most. The palace of Inca Tupaq Yupanqui was where the large church, in the background now sits, so only the Inca foundations remain (how convenient.)

If you move to the left, you will walk down a flight of Inca stairs onto an immense flat area, which the local guides will tell you was a sports training facility. Maybe yes, maybe no. The most important thing though, for our purposes, is that this is the beginning of the exploration of some very amazing stone things to observe and explore. The large wall on your right is most probably of Inca construction, but is also quite finely done, so may be from the Uran Pacha period.

An Uran pacha wall; classic example of their polygonal stone shaping and fitting.

Hanan pacha "throne" with Uran pacha wall behind it.

But what about the above stone outcrop? It looks obviously like Hanan Pacha, and its erosion patterns show that it is much older than the wall just behind it. So if Inca Tupaq Yopanqui built his palace and perhaps the wall, who sculpted this?

This seemingly natural large stone is Hanan pacha; heavily eroded.

And it only gets better from here. The above photo shows a very nicely made wall, at the bottom, that could very well be Inca, but what about the worn large stone above it? Natural? No way, just look at the next photo.

Finely dressed Hanan pacha shaping on this stone.

This gives you a better view of the upper half of the stone outcrop. Focus on the figure in the center of the photo, and then look at the next one.

Carved puma from the Hanan pacha culture; heavily eroded.

That is a carving of a puma, so heavily eroded that if I or someone else had not pointed it out to you, it would be very easy to miss.

Stepped "seats" or "thrones" from the Hanan pacha period.

This is right behind where the above photo was taken; isn't it obvious that the people who built the wall near the church doubtfully made this? Just like at Sachsa uma, where we saw hundreds of these andesite stone outcrops with cube-like sections removed, Chinchero has them in great abundance.

A natural fissure in the rock later shaped by the ancestor.

On the other side of this tunnel/portal are again a multitude of cut out areas; one photograph can not take them all in, but below is a reasonable example.

Hanan pacha stairway leading up to a "throne?"

There are a number of these "throne like" areas, with stairways leading directly to them. Local guides say that this place was sacred for woman; perhaps a place of quiet prayer, where they communed with the moon, Quilla.

After a good night's rest, our next trip is to Ollantaytambo, which I feel should take a full day.

16: Ollantaytambo

Ollantaytambo today, unfortunately, is best known as the jumping off point for Machu picchu, because this is where the main train station is that takes you there. I personally find Ollantaytambo to be, historically speaking, at least as interesting as Machu picchu.

During the Inca period (I hate the term empire) , Ollantaytambo was supposedly the royal estate of Pachacutec, who is said to have conquered the region, then built the town and a ceremonial center. At the time of the Spanish conquest of Peru it served as a stronghold for Manco Inca Yupanqui, leader of the Inca resistance.

The name Ollantaytambo comes from Ollanta and Tambo combined. Ollanta was a high chief, but not full blood Inca, who ruled this area of the Sacred Valley, subordinate to the sapa Inca, about the time of Pachacutec. His great love for a full blood Inca princess was not allowed to "bear fruit" and is the basis of a famous Inca play simply called "Ollanta." Tambo on the other hand is Runa simi for house, and so Ollantaytambo means "the House of Ollanta." He is regarded as being a cousin of the Inca family, and his family name was Anta; a line of great chiefs. Why this place is named after him, and not the sapa Inca remains unclear.

The first site of Ollantaytambo once you pass through the entrance.

Your first view of Ollantaytambo after entering through the gate will be something like the above photo. The Temple of the Sun is on the hill to your left, and the great Inca built terrace system is right in front of you. Very commonly Ollantaytambo is referred to as a fortress, but a fortress against whom is what I question. The only great army that attempted to attack Cusco and the Sacred Valley during Inca times were the Chanka, who were from the south western area called Apurimac. During the reign of Pachacutec they were subdued according to some writers, while others say this occurred, and is more plausible, a century or even two before that.

Ollantaytambo is just one of many examples, with Sachsa uma being the most obvious, where any Inca or pre-Inca structure that has a major wall system, or is located on a hill, is called a "fortress."

View of the main Andene area.

The terraces are more finely built here there almost anywhere else in the Sacred Valley except for, possibly, Pisaq. Instead of just field stones assembled to make andene, here were have much more finely placed and shaped stones. The reason behind this was that it was a place of royalty, that of Pachacutec, and that the corn and other agricultural products produced here were deemed special. This, like Moray, was likely an experimental farm, and the resulting produce were especially bred for the finest qualities of flavour, nutritional value, and hardiness. Being the "garden of the Inca" the seeds from these plants (maize kernels, etc.) were given out as prized gifts to high ranking officials throughout the Tahuantinsuyu; an offering from the "sun of the Sun."

Uran pacha era wall above which is the Sun Temple.

To the left of the main agricultural terraces is the main religious sector, erroneously labelled as a "fortress" by some. In the above photo you see the angled stairway by which you reach this area. The four levels of wall construction to your left, as you ascend, are probably Uran pacha constructions, but possibly only the upper ones, as the lower seem to be of less sophisticated configuration that we attribute to the Inca.

Megalithic pink granite blocks of the Sun Temple.

Here you get your first close glimpse of the Temple or House of the Sun, but once you reach the top, you will see it in its full glory, or at least, with some imagination, see it as it once was. Conventional archaeology says that the Sun Temple was never completed, but fails to say why. It seems to me more likely that this structure was built during Uran Pacha or Hanan Pacha times, and collapsed as the result of a major earthquake.

Multi-ton stone blocks thrown around as if they were childrens' toys.

If you look around, you will see that large pink granite stones, like those in the above photo, are located not just here, but some are also hundreds of feet away. Do you think the builders abandoned this project, or that a catastrophe happened?

The "T" shaped depression which would have held poured bronze.

And, like we saw in the Coricancha, the presence of these t-shaped impressions, that, when two stones were put side by side, would form an "I" shape in which molten bronze was poured to help hold the stones together. A bronze foundry at 11,000 feet elevation? What is left of the Sun Temple is the exquisite wall of 6 stones with a narrow row of shim stones in between. The logic behind the presence of the shim stones is that if a major earthquake occurred, the shims could move, thus absorbing any shock that would shift the larger stones. The fact that this wall still exists in its original form and position is testament to the efficiency and foresight of the builders.

What is left standing of the Sun Temple.

It is only here, in the 600 plus hectares that make up the Ollantaytambo complex, that you find pink granite; the rest being made up of mainly field stones and andesite. The quarry that provided the stones for the Sun Temple's construction lies on the side of a mountain, across the Vilcamayu River, about 5 km downstream at a place called Kachiqhata.

Controversy surrounds not only how the Inca, or earlier Uran or Hanan Pacha cultures were able to move stones of this size down from the quarry, transport them 5 km to Ollantaytambo, after getting them across the river, and then move them up to the top of the hill where they now rest.

The obvious answer given is that slaves did it...funny thing is, where are the references in the chronicles that the Inca had ANY slaves? Ok, then a work force was employed...how many people would be required to move one of these blocks, being say 15 feet long, 6 feet wide and 5 feet thick? If the weight of granite, on average, is 168 pounds per cubic foot, then a block of this size, finished would weigh almost 40 tons. Thor Heyerdahl, in his exploits on Easter

Island, while trying to figure out how the large stone heads there were moved, calculated that on average, across a flat surface and using trees as rollers, it takes 15 people to move a one ton block.

A 30 to 40 ton granite stone shaped with stone hammers and copper chisels?

Based on this calculation, it would take 600 people, fully coordinated, to move a 40 ton block. And this is not taking into account crossing the river, moving it up the hill, or the fact that trees of any size were a rare commodity in Inca times (the forests that you see in and around the Sacred Valley are eucalyptus, brought to Peru from Australia in the 19th century.)

If you wish to climb higher, you can reach the Inti punku, which is an ascent of several hundred more feet. I have personally not been there, and have not found photos that others have taken of it.

The best place to go next is a stroll along the path which leads across the top of the agricultural terraces. This gives you not only a good view of the valley floor below, but leads you to Inca period buildings, most likely used as warehouses, or possibly where agricultural implements were stored.

As you descend, you have a great view of the face of Viracochan, as well as two large buildings, one to the left, and one to the right of his head; we shall get to these later, after we visit the Temple of the Condor!

Andene system with walk way at the top.

This whole area is missed by most visitors, because it is several hundreds yards to the right of the above photo, and most tour guides try to keep you within a fixed time frame of 2 or 3 hours to see the whole area. The Temple of the Condor begins with an amazing wall which has been carved flat, and has interesting protruding stone knobs. It is believed that these, as well as those seen at the Inca Roca wall in Cusco, Coricancha, etc. were used as solar alignment markers.

Solar alignment system beyond the Andene.

Once you walk around the corner, to the right, look up, and you will see the outline of a huge condor in the rock. It is not carved into the rock, but is the hill itself. The head is quite easy to make out, and then the wing, in full form, is to the right.

The path to the Temple of the Condor.

View up at the head and wing of the condor, with Hanan pacha below.

It is quite probable that the condor is natural, and just looks amazingly like a huge bird. But what is not natural are the large and small flat surfaces that were clearly made by people. Not the Inca, because they did not have, as far as we know, the technology required to cut out and polish these andesite areas. So, once again we are led back to the Uran Pacha and Hanan Pacha cultures as being the creators of these.

Hanan pacha "throne" with Sun Temple in the background.

What we also find in this area are various stone blocks and shapes that don't fit with the make up of the nearby Inca walls, or the sculpted andesite surfaces. Some are made of basalt, which is a hard volcanic stone. Anyone who has visited Tiwanaku in Bolivia, or especially the nearby site of Puma punku, will recognize the meticulously sculpted square recesses to be found at the base of the Temple of the Condor as being amazingly similar with the Bolivian sites. These, coupled so to speak with the "T" shaped recesses that we saw up at the Sun temple, suggest that Ollantaytambo and Tiwanaku/Puma punku, as well as the Coricancha in Cusco, were made by the same people, and are perhaps contemporary in terms of time as well.

Square "cut-outs" resembling those seen at Puma punku in Bolivia.

Detail of the amazing workmanship in andesite at the Temple of the Condor.

Beyond this are more Inca terraces, and after that? I have not proceeded far beyond this point, but if you do, and find something of interest, please let me know!

Walking back towards the main area of Ollantaytambo, there are curious stone shapes, which again don't fit in with Inca stone construction, as well as a curious small building.

Entrance to the Virgins of the Sun ceremonial bath.

The four elements: Earth, Air, Fire, and Water.

This little building would seem to have no great symbolic worth, but it does. It is the Temple of the Virgins of the Sun, where they ritually bathed, for purification, at this small fountain. It is here that we find the "four elements" which are important to many cultures around the world: earth, air, fire and water. Earth is the ground you stand on, and the stone of the fountain, air is all around you, the water is rather self evident, and fire is symbolized by the sun, which rises exactly through the center of the window on the solstices.

Hanan pacha of unknown function located between the Sun and Condor Temples.

Another Hanan pacha structure of some kind that most tour guides simply walk past.

The heavy erosion on this large andesite bedrock stone, as well as the sculpted impressions on the other side, are probably not understood by anyone today. However, it is clearly an artefact left behind by the Hanan Pacha culture in my mind.

We know cast our eyes over to the other side of the valley, and the stone mountain that we face. This is called Pinkuylluna, and is where we find Viracochan's profile. The guide Jesus Merello, who is always able to give metaphysical input, explained the entire Ollantaytambo complex to me as being a great example of Inca duality. The Inca thought of almost everything as being part of a dualistic nature; black or white, positive or negative, up or down, male or female, etc.

Ollantaytambo he believes, shows this fully, in that the terraced side is female, with agriculture, fertitlity, etc, and the Pinkuylluna as male, with the face of Viracochan being an aspect of this. The Inca, like many things, probably inherited this duality concept from an earlier and related culture.

View of Pinkuylluna Mountain from the main Ollantaytambo area.

Close up of Pinkuylluna with the face of Viracochan in the center of the photo.

The building to the left of Viracochan's face is his temple, now mainly in ruins. I have not been able to actually climb up to it yet, due to the large "scree" rubble path that is to it's right. There is, however, a path, which is higher up the mountain.

The face of Viracochan (Tunupa) in all of his glory.

On the face, you can clearly make out an eye, with vertical pupil, and the mouth, with a single fang like tooth. If there was a nose, it has seemingly fallen off, and the stone beneath the mouth, as well as vegetation, seems to have been left intact, so as to appear as a beard.

Temple of Viracochan, probably of Inca construction.

Granary on the side of Pinkuylluna Mountain.

This large building, which is in fact a massive granary, which I walked through to reach the small temple shaped like a crown on Viracocha's head, was, by my estimation, of Inca construction, since large megaliths, and sculpted stone shapes are not apparent. There is always wind here, no matter what day and what season, so this building was a perfect place to air dry corn, and desiccate potatoes, for long tern storage. There are also smaller buildings farther to the right, and above these three structures, but their origins and functions are not known to me at this time.

Close up of the crown-like temple on top of Viracochan.

Another interesting features here at Ollantaytambo, which is most likely a natural formation, is the profile of an Inca Face, to the very far left edge of Pinkuylluna.

Profile of the "Inca" on the eastern edge of Pinkuylluna Mountain.

And finally, there are the fountains, which to me show the clearest signs of where the Inca builders venerated earlier Uran Pacha and Hanan Pacha works, by melding their own constructions into them.

One of many fountains with the ancient three step pattern at Ollantaytambo.

In the center is a Hanan Pacha masterwork, to the left is Inca or a more recent repair, and to the right the tight fitting blocks that we know from seeing Uran Pacha works, perhaps the finest being the Coricancha in Cusco.

The magnificence and mystery of the Hanan pacha builders.

Inca street, with central rain trough, in Ollantaytambo.

17: Machu picchu

And now we come to the last, and most famous of Inca sites, Machu picchu. This, the "lost city" of the Inca is known world wide, and is visited by at least 2000 visitors a day. But what is the real story of this place? Who made it, when, and why?

The most common tale of this majestic place was that it was abandoned by the Inca at the time of the Spanish conquest, around 1532 or so, and was lost to the world, becoming completely overgrown with jungle vegetation, until the American archaeologist Hiram Bingham discovered it in 1911. The real story is of course far more complicated than that, and far more intriguing, because during your walk here, you will see constructions that defy the common archaeological theories.

Most guides, and academic publications, will tell you that Machu picchu was simply a jungle clad mountain top prior to the reign of Pachacutec, and it was under his instruction that the whole complex was built between 1438 and 1472, and some assert that it was completed within an even narrower time frame. Theories vary as to its function prior to abandonment, from royal estate, to religious sanctuary, a settlement built to control the economy of conquered regions, a prison for a select few who had committed heinous crimes against Inca society, or even an agricultural experimentation, like Moray.

View of Machu picchu from the end of the Inca Trail.

The true story is most likely, as said earlier, both more interesting and complicated. Pachacutec was most likely the sapa Inca who had the majority of Machu picchu constructed, and made it a place where he could escape from Cusco and rejuvenate. But it was not his private domain, bit more like the equivalent of the modern United States President's Camp David; a place where high officials and advisers from Cusco, and throughout the Tahuantinsuyu would meet to discuss the affairs of state, and be pampered in a beautiful mountain top spa like setting.

The Inca Trail.

The traditional approach to Machu picchu is the present day famous "Inca Trail" which is a very short segment of the Inca road system, traditionally called the Qapaq Nan; great road. It is actually a small tributary that today leads from the town of Urubamba in the Sacred Valley to Machu Picchu itself. The original road originated in Cusco, and the present highway that connects Cusco and Urubamba was also part of this Inca Trail originally.

Visitors today approach Machu picchu by way of a "switch back" road, constructed in the early 20th century; an access for archaeolological crews.

View of Machu picchu and the zig zag bus road to it.

The original road is very narrow, and lends evidence to the idea that Machu picchu was a very important place for conducting governmental affairs, thus had very limited access. This could also explain why the location of the site faded from local consciousness after it was abandoned; it would be easy for the jungle to

quickly erase the road from view. The only other well known access to Machu picchu is a very narrow trail that hugs the side of the hills below it, and reaches the site on it's western side. The drawbridge adds further evidence that access to the area was highly restricted.

The alternate route to Machu picchu with wooden draw bridge.

The drawbridge is made of roughly shaped stones, reasonably well fitted together, so this is most likely Inca construction, and not that of an earlier culture.

As has been said, Hiram Bingham was the first person to expose Machu picchu to the world, through National Geographic Society sponsorship and exposure in their famed magazine; in fact, they devoted the entire April 1913 issue to Machu picchu. But he hardly "discovered it." An American historian employed as a lecturer at Yale University, Bingham had been searching for the city of Vilcabamba, which was the last Inca refuge during the Spanish conquest. He had worked for years in previous trips and explorations around the zone, and it was Pablito Alvarez, a local 11 year-old local Quechua speaking Native boy, led Bingham up to Machu Picchu.

The site was not completely covered in vegetation as I have said. In fact, Bingham stumbled across two native farmers, named Richarte and Alvarez, who had cleared some of the Inca terraces and had been growing potatoes, corn, sugarcane and other crops there for 3 or 4 years, and were living there, possibly full time.

Also, other adventurers had been there before Bingham. . Simone Waisbard, a long-time researcher from Cusco, claims that Enrique Palma, Gabino Sánchez, and Agustín Lizárraga left their names engraved on one of the rocks at Machu Picchu on 14 July 1901. Also in 1904, an engineer named Franklin supposedly spotted the ruins from a distant mountain. He told Thomas Payne, an English Christian missionary living in the region, about the site, Payne's family members claim. They also report that in 1906, Payne and fellow missionary Stuart E. McNairn (1867–1956) climbed up to the ruins.

The site may have been discovered and plundered in 1867 by a German businessman, Augusto Berns. There is some evidence that a German engineer, J. M. von Hassel, arrived earlier. Maps found by historians show references to Machu Picchu as early as 1874.

And the question arises, why was Machu picchu abandoned? The obvious answer is that the Spanish had arrived, and so this special place was abandoned so that they would not find it. But that is too simple an answer. What is more probable is that it was the victim of that, introduced diseases, and the Inca civil war which had just preceded the Spanish conquest. Oral traditions indicate that Machu picchu was, in its capacity as a spa and resting place for the Inca and officials, also a medical experimental place.

It is said that the medical personnel there were using snake venom in order to cure diseases, and extend human life expectancy. This could of course be a fable, but the story is intriguing. What is said is that the officials who were staying at Machu picchu at the time of the civil war between the full blood Inca Huascar, and the half-blood from Ecuador, Atahuallpa, were on Huascar's side of the conflict, because he was the true leader.

Atahaullpa wished to conquer the entire Tahuantinsuyu, and wanted all full blood Inca, as well as Inca officials killed. Upon this news reaching Machu picchu via the Inca runners, the Chasqui, all personnel decided to abandon the site. The evacuation is also said to be in conjunction with the fact that news had reached them of a mysterious group of humans who had just landed on the north coast near Tumbes, and brought death with them.

The diseases which became plagues had preceded the arrival of the Spanish, by moving through the Native populations from the north, starting in Panama, where the Spanish had an early settlement. Supposedly, the last act that the inhabitants performed, was the release of the poisonous snakes that they were keeping for experimental purposes. That could be the reason why the local people didn't necessarily forget about Machu picchu's existence, they simply considered it a dangerous place.

Your first view of Machu picchu beyond the tourist entrance.

This is what greets you as you enter through the main gate. The simplest way to see Machu picchu is by making a clock wise route through the whole complex. This gate is not the traditional entrance as used by the Inca; you are actually entering onto the beginning of the main agricultural terrace (Andene) system, and the buildings here are thought to have been either workers houses, or where farming tools were stored.

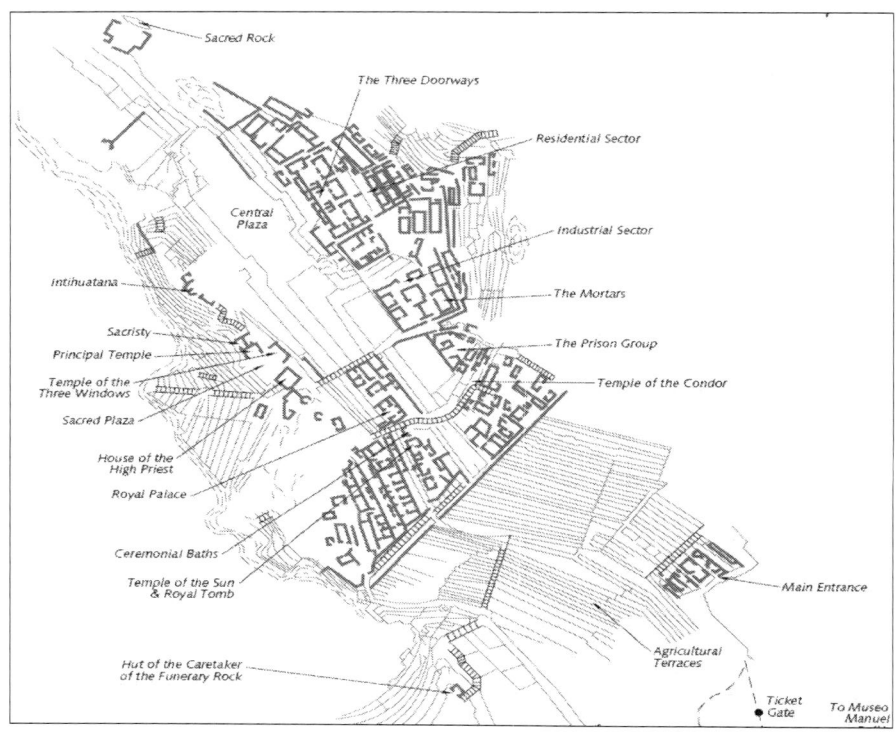

Diagram of the Machu picchu complex.

The traditional entrance, via the Inca Trail, takes you into the city just below the "Hut of the Caretaker." Before we actually begin the tour, please take into account that many of the names and functions of buildings and spaces at Machu picchu are speculation, based on the observations and thoughts mainly of Hiram Bingham, who is not believed to have consulted much with oral tradition experts. But then again, who could he have consulted with, as few people theoretically had knowledge of it's existence since the 16th century.

Our tour may stray from the conventional one given by most guides, and in fact it already has, but it is based on melding oral and conventional histories together, as much as is possible.

Looking back at the entrance and gardeners' houses at Machu picchu.

We walk along the Inca made terraces to reach the first main set of stairs, which takes us up, and to the left. It is from here, near the "Hut of the Caretaker" that we get the first true view of the whole city.

Stairway up through the Andene to the "Hut of the Caretaker."

"Hut of the Caretaker" with Huayna picchu Mountain in the background.

The "Funerary Rock" is clearly from the Hanan pacha period.

The so-called Funerary Rock was described to me by a Peruvian guide as being a place of human sacrifice. "To whom or what" I asked? "To ensure a good harvest and sufficient rain" I was told. Really, so a culture that had the Moray experimental farm, over 200 varieties of potatoes, for example, bred to live in any possible climatic condition in the Tahuantinsuyu, massive Andene systems fed with ingenious aqueduct and other irrigations systems fed by both glaciers and rain water, still needed human sacrifice to ensure good crops? What nonsense.

It is far more likely that this stone, shaped out of andesite and with steps, niches, and a flat surface that comfortably could fit a prone person, was a place of meditation, built long before the Inca, by the Hanan Pacha culture. This is the first obvious example at Machu picchu where we find evidence of an earlier culture.

The western side of Machu picchu showing amazing Andene.

We descend down from this vantage point and what is probably the main section of the oldest area of Machu picchu. This statement is based on the fact that we find the finest stone workmanship here; clear examples of the Uran and Hanan Pacha cultures. I will become readily obvious to your eyes.

Doorway from the Uran Pacha period.

The above doorway is a case in point; notice how the finest construction is around the door itself, and the areas above and to the left are of poorer and clearly later construction, as if it was repaired.

Walled enclosure of the Sun Temple.

The Temple of the Sun is believed to have been used by the Inca as a solar calendar, because on the solstices, at sunrise, the sun enters a specific window and strikes a line carved into a stone bedrock slab. What most guides won't tell you is that the circular temple was not built by the Inca; it's clearly Uran pacha by the exactness of the masonry. What's more, the stone that it is enclosing is older still, Hanan pacha.

Thus, the Temple of the Sun was inherited from the Uran pacha who in turn inherited it from the Hanan pacha.

The Hanan pacha Sun Temple rock with Uran pacha circular wall around it.

Cave system under the Sun Temple with Hanan pacha stair system.

It is under the Temple of the Sun that we find more Hanan pacha; a stone stairway that ends at a flat wall, and supposed evidence of a royal tomb; however, where are the royal remains? Since all of the artefacts found by Hiram Bingham and his National Geographic financed crew are now housed at the Peabody Museum at the University of Yale; perhaps only they presently know.

The next famous place is the Temple of the Three Windows, which is another beautiful example of Uran pacha construction.

Exterior of the Temple of the Three Windows.

This is more or less the entrance to the main oldest section of Machu picchu, as you can witness from the plethora of amazing tight fitting stone work from this point up to the Intihuatana.

Inside the Temple of the Three Windows; Uran pacha.

From the inside of the Temple of the Three Windows, to your left, is the stairway which takes you up to the Intihuatana, the most famous and also most enigmatic stone monument at Machu picchu, and perhaps all of South America.

Entrance to the Intihuatana area; Hanan pacha.

It is loosely translated to be the "Hitching Post of the Sun" and an explanation of what that in fact means is important here. On each solstice, in December and June, about the 22nd of the month, the sun stops drifting to the right on its daily movement, and seems to stay that way for three days, until the 25th, when it starts to move back again. During this time period, it seems to "sit" in relation to the Intihuatana, as if it is fixed or tied there.

In this way, the Intihuatana would tell the Inca astronomers and priests that the solstice had arrived. This was of course important for ritual reasons, as well as agricultural timing. But the Intihuatana is far more complicated and mysterious than that.

Intihuatana; looking at its eastern side.

Looking at the southern side of the Intihuatana.

The four corners of the Intihuatana also point to the four cardinal directions of north, south, east and west, and what is amazing, is that there are four mountain peaks that correspond to these alignments. Furthermore, on the top of each peak is an Intihuatana. Are we really to believe that the Inca went to all of that trouble in order to have an instrument that told them what time of year it was?

I have not been able to find out from any source who made the other Intihuatanas or why they are in their exacting locations, but suspect that they, along with the beautiful stone work in the above photos was made by an older culture, the Hanan pacha, who we know almost nothing about, except that they built megalithic works from bedrock. Such is the case of this Intihuatana, and also the one at Pisaq; they were not brought from another location, but are outcrops of the earth itself.

But why was this important? The most logical answer that comes to mind is that the Intihuatana had to be fixed exactly in place, and not move, whether by human hands or earthquakes, to insure that its markings stayed true through time, indeed possibly millennia.

Facing Huayna picchu.

An even more intriguing minor aspect, in terms of a mark on the stone, is that at the upper edge corner, which faces north, is an indentation which most people are never told about. What it is, are you ready for this? It points to magnetic north. But why you, and most other people will ask, did the Inca need this? Again, the Inca probably did not construct it, and the Hanan pacha who most likely did, must have had a reason.

Descending down the staircase, to the Huayna picchu side of the Intihuatana, brings you to the main plaza of Machu picchu. From here, you walk straight towards Huayna picchu until you reach the gate which allows to to hike up the 2000 stone steps to the top of the "Young Bird" should you be the first of 400 people to be the first each day to sign up. However, should the quota already be full for the day, or while you are pondering the 2000 stairs, have a look to your right...

A portion of the central courtyard.

The "Sacred Rock" near the entrance to the Huyana picchu stairways.

The so-called Sacred Rock, as you can see in this photo, looks quite natural in appearance. Why it has the name that it does I have never found out. But what is intriguing about it is that it's shape does reflect the background; the contours do, in some ways look like the background. The presence of a finely made wall surrounding it does show that it was revered; and the quite tight fit of the stones could be that of the Inca, or possibly the Uran pacha culture.

Ok, so you are either ready to ascend up to Huayna picchu, or have been told that you are guest number 401; in either case, here is a brief snapshot of the place.

Magnificent Huyana picchu.

What many people don't realize is that Huayna picchu is not simply a mountain. The reason why there are stairs, all 2000 of them, that lead you to the top is the fact that there is a large complex of buildings encircling the summit, with enough Andene to feed many cliff top inhabitants. In fact, the top of Huayna picchu was so well provisioned, that several Inca, or even earlier people, could have happily lived up there without ever having to come down!

Buildings and Andene on top of Huayna picchu.

But what would have been its function? The obvious, but most typical and boring explanation would be that it was a military lookout for detecting the presence of possible invaders, but, who would that have been? Natives from the jungle? A southern force that had made it past all of the Inca defenses in the Sacred Valley, including at Sachsayhuaman?

More likely, it was a place where spiritual advisers or even astronomer priests lived; the two quite possibly being one and the same. Contrary to the western world and it's compartmentalization of roles and careers, in the Inca scheme of things, cosmology and religion were very much interlinked. The sun, Inti, was the physical manifestation of the divine source, Viracocha; the moon, Quilla (or Killa) was the female aspect, and different star systems formed the shapes of animals; llama, frog, serpent, etc.

One of the caves that you climb through on your ascent.

The way up is worth the effort, because at the top you get an incredible panorama of the entire Machu picchu complex. And it is from here that you also see that Machu picchu was designed in the shape of an enormous condor, its head facing west.

Machu picchu as seen from the top of Huana Picchu.

Condor eye view of the great city shaped like...a condor!

If you still have energy, and are still adventurous, follow the sign from the top of Huayna picchu that leads you down the back side. Through a series of trails, stone stairs, and ladders you make it half way down the mountain to the Temple of the Moon; most likely a place of pilgrimage for Virgins of the Sun.

The way down to the Temple of the Moon.

Inca period buildings near the Temple of the Moon.

The author on a Hanan pacha "throne" in the Temple of the Moon."

View from the "throne."

The masonry here is immaculate; perhaps the best that exists in the Machu picchu area, and also shows us that the earlier cultures were here before the Inca; the Uran pacha constructing the tight fitting rock wall and enclosure structures, and the Hanan pacha the megalithic single stone works, such as the seat that I sat on.

There are agricultural terraces here, enough, like at the peak of Huayna Picchu, to feed quite a few people. So it too may have been a place where devotees could have lived for extensive periods of time without having to leave back to the main Machu picchu area.

The walk, or should I say hike back to the main area, to your right, is less challenging than the way down, but not easy by any means. Remembering that you are still at about 10,000 feet or so of altitude, your heart sounds out the upward effort.

Stone walkway back to Machu picchu.

View of Machu picchu proper from the trail leading from the Temple of the Moon.

trail winds back through the eastern side of Machu picchu's buildings and squares. The most interesting place in the area, I think, is the Temple of the Condor, which is also close to the end of out tour.

Temple of the Condor.

The tear drop shape in the main stone is said to represent the head of the condor, and the two curved stones the white ring that encircles it's neck.

Close up of the "head and neck" of the Hanan pacha Temple of the Condor.

It's function? Again, most sources say "ritual purposes" which is as vague as one can be. I honestly have not been able to find real details as to what the function of this place was during Inca times, and before the Inca got here. In some ways that is good, as mysteries prompt one to "dig" deeper. Back towards the entrance we must now walk...

The sad trip back to the entrance gate...

And so now we leave Machu picchu, having not seen everything, nor revealed every secret of the place, but have learned much more than the average tour of the area gives. And as a teaser for future study, Machu picchu is of course not the traditional, ancient name for this area. Hiram Bingham chose to name it after the mountain on which it resides, or more specifically, the one that rises to the south side, and along which the Inca trail clings.

The traditional name for this sacred space is Yllampu, which in Runa simi means "The Resting Place of the Gods." Quite appropriate I think...

Other places in the area which are well worth visiting include those which Hiram Bingham saw prior to his "discovery" of Machu picchu. None of these sites are especially easy to get to, and are expensive in terms and money as well as time. However, for the intrepid traveler, or even arm chair explorer, here are glimpses of other sacred spaces:

The Inca Trail to Choquequirao.

View of the main complex.

Choqequirao, the Cradle of Gold in Runa simi, is located south west of Cusco in the Apurimac region near the town of Abancay. Choquequirao's builder, Topa Inca, chose his city's site and design precisely because of the similarities to Machu Picchu., or so the story goes. The two cities were about the same size and served the same religious, political and agricultural functions. But because archaeologists long underestimated the importance of Choquequirao, the city's existence was known for almost 300 years before the first restoration was begun in 1993. It is still only 30 percent uncovered. The Peruvian government is just beginning to plan for large-scale tourism there. Yuck!

View of the strange flat topped hill near the main complex.

Llama images in the Inca period Andene.

Magnificent example of Hanan pacha, showing that they preceded the Inca here.

The presence of Hanan pacha works such as the one above shows that Choquequirao, like Machu picchu (Yllampu) was inhabited long before the Inca arrived. The marauding Spanish conquistadors missed this one too...

Hanan pachu construction at Vilcabamba, said to be sacred to the Virgins of the Sun.

Vilcabamba (Sacred Plain)was a city where Manco Inca, the younger brother of the last true sapa Inca Huascar retreated to in 1539 when he escaped Spanish imprisonment and was the last refuge of the Inca until it fell to the Spaniards in 1572, signaling the end of Inca resistance to Spanish rule.

After the Incan empire fell, the city was burned and the area swiftly became a remote, secluded spot of Peru. The location of Vilcabamba was forgotten. The first outsiders in modern times to come to the remote forest site that has since come to be identified with Vilcabamba la Vieja were three *Cuzqueños*: Manuel Ugarte, Manuel Lopez Torres, and Juan Cancio Saavedra, in 1892. The site of the ruins of the city were then rediscovered by Hiram Bingham in 1911 at the remote forest site 130 kilometres (81 mi) west of Cusco called Espíritu Pampu, and are written of in his classic *Lost City of the Incas*.

Inca period buildings of Vilcabamba.

The "White Rock" also known as Chuchipalta is a Hanan pacha structure near Vilcabamba.

Hanan pacha work at Vitcos, close to Vilcabamba.

Hanan pacha masterpiece near Saihuite, near Abancay, south west of Cusco.

Enigmatic stone at Saihuite, near Abancay; unknown age, unknown creator...

Printed in Great Britain
by Amazon